PENGUIN B

The Sta

Jacob Burckhardt

1818–1897

Jacob Burckhardt

The State as a Work of Art

PENGUIN BOOKS — GREAT IDEAS

PENGUIN BOOKS

Published by the Penguin Group
Penguin Books Ltd, 80 Strand, London WC2R 0RL, England
Penguin Group (USA) Inc., 375 Hudson Street, New York, New York 10014, USA
Penguin Group (Canada), 90 Eglinton Avenue East, Suite 700, Toronto, Ontario, Canada M4P 2Y3
(a division of Pearson Penguin Canada Inc.)
Penguin Ireland, 25 St Stephen's Green, Dublin 2, Ireland (a division of Penguin Books Ltd)
Penguin Group (Australia), 250 Camberwell Road, Camberwell, Victoria 3124, Australia
(a division of Pearson Australia Group Pty Ltd)
Penguin Books India Pvt Ltd, 11 Community Centre, Panchsheel Park,
New Delhi – 110 017, India
Penguin Group (NZ), 67 Apollo Drive, Rosedale, North Shore 0632, New Zealand
(a division of Pearson New Zealand Ltd)
Penguin Books (South Africa) (Pty) Ltd, 24 Sturdee Avenue, Rosebank, Johannesburg 2196,
South Africa

Penguin Books Ltd, Registered Offices: 80 Strand, London WC2R 0RL, England

www.penguin.com

Taken from *The Civilization of the Renaissance in Italy*, published by Penguin Classics 1990
This selection published in Penguin Books 2010

1

Set in 11/13 Dante MT Std
Typeset by TexTech International
Printed in England by Clays Ltd, St Ives plc

ISBN: 978-0-141-04811-6

Contents

Introduction

This work bears the title of an essay in the strictest sense of the word. No one is more conscious than the writer with what limited means and strength he has addressed himself to a task so arduous. And even if he could look with greater confidence upon his own researches, he would hardly thereby feel more assured of the approval of competent judges. To each eye, perhaps, the outlines of a given civilization present a different picture; and in treating of a civilization which is the mother of our own, and whose influence is still at work among us, it is unavoidable that individual judgement and feeling should tell every moment both on the writer and on the reader. In the wide ocean upon which we venture, the possible ways and directions are many; and the same studies which have served for this work might easily, in other hands, not only receive a wholly different treatment and application, but lead also to essentially different conclusions. Such indeed is the importance of the subject, that it still calls for fresh investigation, and may be studied with advantage from the most varied points of view. Meanwhile we are content if a patient hearing is granted us, and if this book be taken and judged as a whole. It is the most serious difficulty of the history of civilization that a great intellectual process must be broken up into single, and often into what seem arbitrary categories, in order to be in any way intelligible. It was formerly our intention to fill up the gaps in this book by a special work on the art of the Renaissance – an intention, however, which we have been able to fulfil only in part. The struggle between the popes and the Hohenstaufen left Italy in a political condition which differed essentially from that of other countries of the West. While in France, Spain and England the feudal system was so organized that, at the close of its existence, it was naturally transformed into a unified monarchy, and while in Germany it helped to maintain, at least outwardly, the unity of the empire, Italy had shaken it off almost entirely. The emperors of the fourteenth century, even in the most favourable case, were no longer received and respected as feudal lords, but as possible leaders and supporters of powers already in existence; while the papacy, with its creatures and allies, was strong enough to hinder national unity in the future, not strong enough itself to bring about that unity. Between the two lay a multitude of political units – republics and despots – in part of long standing, in part of recent origin, whose existence was founded simply on their power to maintain it. In them for the first time we detect the modern political spirit of Europe, surrendered freely to its own instincts, often displaying the worst features of an unbridled egotism, outraging every right, and killing every germ of a healthier culture. But, wherever this vicious tendency is overcome or in any way compensated, a new fact appears in history – the state as the outcome of reflection and calculation, the state as a work of art. This new life displays itself in a hundred forms, both in the republican and in the despotic states, and determines their inward constitution, no less than their foreign policy. We shall limit ourselves to the consideration of the completer and more clearly defined type, which is offered by the despotic states.

The internal condition of the despotically governed states had a memorable counterpart in the Norman empire of Lower Italy and Sicily, after its transformation by the emperor Frederick II. Bred amid treason and peril in the neighbourhood of the Saracens, Frederick, the first ruler of the modern type who sat upon a throne, had early accustomed himself to a thoroughly objective treatment of affairs. His acquaintance with the internal condition and administration of the Saracenic states was close and intimate; and the mortal struggle in which he was engaged with the papacy compelled him, no less than his adversaries, to bring into the field all the resources at his command. Frederick's measures (especially after the year 1231) are aimed at the complete destruction of the feudal state, at the transformation of the people into a multitude destitute of will and of the means of resistance, but profitable in the utmost degree to the exchequer. He centralized, in a manner hitherto unknown in the West, the whole judicial and political administration. No office was henceforth to be filled by popular election, under penalty of the devastation of the offending district and of the enslavement of its inhabitants. The taxes, based on a comprehensive assessment, and distributed in accordance with Muhammadan usages, were collected by those cruel and vexatious methods without which, it is true, it is impossible to obtain any money from Orientals. Here, in short, we find, not a people, but simply a disciplined multitude of subjects, who were forbidden, for example, to marry out of the country without special permission, and under no circumstances were allowed to study abroad. The university of Naples was the first we know of to restrict the freedom of study, while the East, in these respects at all events, left its youth unfettered. It was after the example of Muhammadan rules that Frederick traded on his own account in all parts of the Mediterranean, reserving to himself the monopoly of many commodities, and restricting in various ways the commerce of his subjects. The Fatimite Caliphs, with all their esoteric unbelief, were, at least in their earlier history, tolerant of all the differences in the religious faith of their people; Frederick, on the other hand, crowned his system of government by a religious inquisition, which will seem the more reprehensible when we remember that in the persons of the heretics he was persecuting the representatives of a free municipal life. Lastly, the internal police, and the kernel of the army for foreign service, was composed of Saracens who had been brought over from Sicily to Nocera and Lucera – men who were deaf to the cry of misery and careless of the ban of the Church. At a later period the subjects, by whom the use of weapons had long been forgotten, were passive witnesses of the fall of Manfred and of the seizure of the government by Charles of Anjou; the latter continued to use the system which he found already at work.

At the side of the centralizing emperor appeared a usurper of the most peculiar kind: his vicar and son-in-law, Ezzelino da Romano. He stands as the representative of no system of government or administration, for all his activity was wasted in struggles for supremacy in the eastern part of Upper Italy; but as a political type he was a figure of no less importance for the future than his imperial protector Frederick. The conquests and usurpations which had hitherto taken place in the Middle Ages rested on real or pretended inheritance and other such claims, or else were effected against unbelievers and excommunicated persons. Here for the first time the attempt was openly made to found a throne by wholesale murder and endless barbarities, by the adoption, in short, of any means with a view to nothing but the end pursued. None of his successors, not even Cesare Borgia, rivalled the colossal guilt of Ezzelino; but the example once set was not forgotten, and his fall led to no return of justice among the nations, and served as no warning to future transgressors.

It was in vain at such a time that St Thomas Aquinas, a born subject of Frederick, set up the theory of a constitutional monarchy, in which the prince was to be supported by an upper house named by himself, and a representative body elected by the people. Such theories found no echo outside the lecture-room, and Frederick and Ezzelino were and remain for Italy the great political phenomena of the thirteenth century. Their personality, already half legendary, forms the most important subject of *The Hundred Old Tales*, whose original composition falls certainly within this century. In them Ezzelino is spoken of with the awe which all mighty impressions leave behind them. His person became the centre of a whole literature from the chronicle of eye-witnesses to the half-mystical tragedy of later poets.

Despots of the Fourteenth Century

The tyrannies, great and small, of the fourteenth century afford constant proof that examples such as these were not thrown away. Their misdeeds cried forth loudly and have been circumstantially told by historians. As states depending for existence on themselves alone, and scientifically organized with a view to this object, they present to us a higher interest than that of mere narrative.

The deliberate adaptation of means to ends, of which no prince out of Italy had at that time a conception, joined to almost absolute power within the limits of the state, produced among the despots both men and modes of life of a peculiar character. The chief secret of government in the hands of the prudent ruler lay in leaving the incidence of taxation so far as possible where he found it, or as he had first arranged it. The chief sources of income were: a land tax, based on a valuation; definite taxes on articles of consumption and duties on exported and imported goods; together with the private fortune of the ruling house. The only possible increase was derived from the growth of business and of general prosperity. Loans, such as we find in the free cities, were here unknown; a well-planned confiscation was held a preferable means of raising money, provided only that it left public credit unshaken – an end attained, for example, by the truly oriental practice of deposing and plundering the director of the finances.

Out of this income the expenses of the little court, of the bodyguard, of the mercenary troops, and of the public buildings were met, as well as of the buffoons and men of talent who belonged to the personal attendants of the prince. The illegitimacy of his rule isolated the tyrant and surrounded him with constant danger; the most honourable alliance which he could form was with intellectual merit, without regard to its origin. The liberality of the northern princes of the thirteenth century was confined to the knights, to the nobility which served and sang. It was otherwise with the Italian despot. With his thirst for fame and his passion for monumental works, it was talent, not birth, which he needed. In the company of the poet and the scholar he felt himself in a new position, almost, indeed in possession of a new legitimacy.

No prince was more famous in this respect than the ruler of Verona, Can Grande della Scala, who numbered among the illustrious exiles whom he entertained at his court representatives of the whole of Italy. The men of letters were not ungrateful. Petrarch, whose visits at the courts of such men have been so severely censured, sketched an ideal picture of a prince of the fourteenth century. He demands great things from his patron, the lord of Padua, but in a manner which shows that he holds him capable of them.

> Thou must not be the master but the father of thy subjects, and must love them as thy children; yea, as members of thy body. Weapons, guards and soldiers thou mayest employ against the enemy – with thy subjects goodwill is sufficient. By citizens, of course, I mean

those who love the existing order; for those who daily desire change are rebels and traitors, and against such a stern justice may take its course.

Here follows, worked out in detail, the purely modern fiction of the omnipotence of the state. The prince is to take everything into his charge, to maintain and restore churches and public buildings, to keep up the municipal police, to drain the marshes, to look after the supply of wine and corn; so to distribute the taxes that the people can recognize their necessity; he is to support the sick and the helpless, and to give his protection and society to distinguished scholars, on whom his fame in after ages will depend.

But whatever might be the brighter sides of the system, and the merits of individual rulers, yet the men of the fourteenth century were not without a more or less distinct consciousness of the brief and uncertain tenure of most of these despotisms. Inasmuch as political institutions like these are naturally secure in proportion to the size of the territory in which they exist, the larger principalities were constantly tempted to swallow up the smaller. Whole hecatombs of petty rulers were sacrificed at this time to the Visconti alone. As a result of this outward danger an inward ferment was in ceaseless activity; and the effect of the situation on the character of the ruler was generally of the most sinister kind. Absolute power, with its temptations to luxury and unbridled selfishness, and the perils to which he was exposed from enemies and conspirators, turned him almost inevitably into a tyrant in the worst sense of the word. Well for him if he could trust his nearest relations! But where all was illegitimate, there could be no regular law of inheritance, either with regard to the succession or to the division of the ruler's property; and consequently the heir, if incompetent or a minor, was liable in the interest of the family itself to be supplanted by an uncle or cousin of more resolute character. The acknowledgement or exclusion of the bastards was a fruitful source of contest; and most of these families in consequence were plagued with a crowd of discontented and vindictive kinsmen. This circumstance gave rise to continual outbreaks of treason and to frightful scenes of domestic bloodshed. Sometimes the pretenders lived abroad in exile, and like the Visconti, who practised the fisherman's craft on the Lake of Garda, viewed the situation with patient indifference. When asked by a messenger of his rival when and how he thought of returning to Milan, one gave the reply, 'By the same means as those by which I was expelled, but not till his crimes have outweighed my own.' Sometimes, too, the despot was sacrificed by his relations, with the view of saving the family, to the public conscience which he had too grossly outraged. In a few cases the government was in the hands of the whole family, or at least the ruler was bound to take their advice; and here, too, the distribution of property and influence often led to bitter disputes.

The whole of this system excited the deep and persistent hatred of the Florentine writers of that epoch. Even the pomp and display, with which the despot was perhaps less anxious to gratify his own vanity than to impress the popular imagination, awakened their keenest sarcasm. Woe to an adventurer if he fell into their hands, like the upstart Doge Agnello of Pisa (1364), who used to ride out with a golden sceptre, and show himself at the window of his house, 'as relics are shown', reclining on embroidered drapery and cushions, served like a pope or emperor, by kneeling attendants. More often, however, the old Florentines speak on this subject in a tone of lofty seriousness. Dante saw and characterized well the vulgarity and commonplace which marked the ambition of the new princes. 'What mean their trumpets and their bells, their horns and their flutes; but come, hangman – come, vultures?' The castle of the tyrant, as pictured by the popular mind, is a lofty and solitary building, full of dungeons and listening-tubes, the home of cruelty and misery. Misfortune is foretold to all who enter the service of the despot, who even becomes at last himself an object of pity: he must needs be the enemy of all good and honest men; he can trust no one, and can read in the faces of his subjects the expectation of his fall. 'As despotisms rise, grow, and are consolidated, so grows in their midst the hidden element which must produce their dissolution and ruin.' But the deepest ground of dislike has not been stated; Florence was then the scene of the richest development of human individuality, while for the despots no other individuality could be suffered to live and thrive but their own and that of their nearest dependants. The control of the individual was rigorously carried out, even down to the establishment of a system of passports.

The astrological superstitions and the religious unbelief of many of the tyrants gave, in the minds of their contemporaries, a peculiar colour to this awful and God-forsaken existence. When the last Carrara could no longer defend the walls and gates of the plague-stricken Padua, hemmed in on all sides by the Venetians (1405), the soldiers of the guard heard him cry to the devil 'to come and kill me'.

The most complete and instructive type of the tyranny of the fourteenth century is to be found unquestionably among the Visconti of Milan, from the death of the Archbishop Giovanni onwards (1354). The family likeness which shows itself between Bernabò and the worst of the Roman emperors is unmistakable; the most important public object was the prince's boar-hunting; whoever interfered with it was put to death with torture; the terrified people were forced to maintain 5,000 boar-hounds, with strict responsibility for their health and safety. The taxes were extorted by every conceivable sort of compulsion; seven daughters of the prince received a dowry of 100,000 gold florins apiece; and an enormous treasure was collected. On the death of his wife (1384) an order was issued 'to the subjects' to share his grief, as once they had shared his joy, and to wear mourning for a year. The *coup de main* (1385) by which his nephew Giangaleazzo got him into his power – one of those brilliant plots which make the heart of even late historians beat more quickly – was strikingly characteristic of the man.

In Giangaleazzo that passion for the colossal which was common to most of the despots shows itself on the largest scale. He undertook, at the cost of 300,000 golden florins, the construction of gigantic dykes, to divert in case of need the Mincio from Mantua and the Brenta from Padua, and thus to render these cities defenceless. It is not impossible, indeed, that he thought of draining away the lagoons of Venice. He founded that most wonderful of all convents, the Certosa of Pavia, and the cathedral of Milan, 'which exceeds in size and splendour all the churches of Christendom'. The Palace in Pavia, which his father Galeazzo began and which he himself finished, was probably by far the most magnificent of the princely dwellings of Europe. There he transferred his famous library, and the great collection of relics of the saints, in which he placed a peculiar faith. It would have been strange indeed if a prince of this character had not also cherished the highest ambitions in political matters. King Wenceslaus made him Duke (1395); he was hoping for nothing less than the kingdom of Italy or the imperial crown, when (1402) he fell ill and died. His whole territories are said to have paid him in a single year, besides the regular contribution of 1,200,000 gold florins, no less than 800,000 more in extraordinary subsidies. After his death the dominions which he had brought together by every sort of violence fell to pieces; and for a time even the original nucleus could with difficulty be maintained by his successors. What might have become of his sons Giovanni Maria (died 1412) and Filippo Maria (died 1417), had they lived in a different country and among other traditions, cannot be said. But, as heirs of their house, they inherited that monstrous capital of cruelty and cowardice which had been accumulated from generation to generation.

Giovanni Maria, too, is famed for his dogs, which were no longer, however, used for hunting but for tearing human bodies. Tradition has preserved their names, like those of the bears of the Emperor Valentinian I. In May

1409, when war was going on, and the starving populace cried to him in the streets, *Pace! Pace!*, he let loose his mercenaries upon them, and 200 lives were sacrificed; under penalty of the gallows it was forbidden to utter the words *pace* and *guerra*, and the priests were ordered, instead of *dona nobis pacem*, to say *tranquillitatem*. At last a band of conspirators took advantage of the moment when Facino Cane, the chief *condottiere* of the insane ruler, lay ill at Pavia, and cut down Giovanni Maria in the church of San Gottardo at Milan; the dying Facino on the same day made his officers swear to stand by the heir Filippo Maria, whom he himself urged his wife to take for a second husband. His wife, Beatrice di Tenda, followed his advice. We shall have occasion to speak of Filippo Maria later on.

And in times like these Cola di Rienzi was dreaming of founding on the rickety enthusiasm of the corrupt population of Rome a new state which was to comprise all Italy. By the side of rulers such as those whom we have described, he seems no better than a poor deluded fool.

Despots of the Fifteenth Century

The despotisms of the fifteenth century show an altered character. Many of the less important tyrants, and some of the greater, like the Scala and the Carrara, had disappeared, while the more powerful ones, aggrandized by conquest, had given to their systems each its characteristic development. Naples, for example, received a fresh and stronger impulse from the new Aragonese dynasty. A striking feature of this epoch is the attempt of the *condottieri* to found independent dynasties of their own. Facts and the actual relations of things, apart from traditional estimates, are alone regarded; talent and audacity win the great prizes. The petty despots, to secure a trustworthy support, begin to enter the service of the larger states, and become themselves *condottieri*, receiving in return for their services money and impunity for their misdeeds, if not an increase of territory. All, whether small or great, must exert themselves more, must act with greater caution and calculation, and must learn to refrain from too wholesale barbarities; only so much wrong is permitted by public opinion as is necessary for the end in view, and this the impartial bystander certainly finds no fault with. No trace is here visible of that half-religious loyalty by which the legitimate princes of the West were supported; personal popularity is the nearest approach we can find to it. Talent and calculation are the only means of advancement. A character like that of Charles the Bold, which wore itself out in the passionate pursuit of impracticable ends, was a riddle to the Italians. 'The Swiss were only peasants, and if they were all killed, that would be no satisfaction for the Burgundian nobles who might fall in the war. If the duke got possession of all Switzerland without a struggle, his income would not be 5,000 ducats the greater.' The medieval features in the character of Charles, his chivalrous aspirations and ideals, had long become unintelligible to the Italians. The diplomatists of the South, when they saw him strike his officers and yet keep them in his service, when he maltreated his troops to punish them for a defeat, and then threw the blame on his counsellors in the presence of the same troops, gave him up for lost. Louis XI, on the other hand, whose policy surpasses that of the Italian princes in their own style, and who was an avowed admirer of Francesco Sforza, must be placed in all that regards culture and refinement far below these rulers.

Good and evil lie strangely mixed together in the Italian states of the fifteenth century. The personality of the ruler is so highly developed, often of such deep significance, and so characteristic of the conditions and needs of the time, that to form an adequate moral judgement on it is no easy task.

The foundation of the system was and remained illegitimate, and nothing could remove the curse which rested upon it. The imperial approval or investiture made no change in the matter, since the people attached little weight to the fact that the despot had bought a piece of parchment somewhere in foreign countries, or from some stranger passing through his territory. If the emperor had been good for anything – so ran the logic of uncritical common sense – he would never have let the tyrant rise at all. Since the Roman expedition of Charles IV, the emperors had done nothing more in Italy than sanction a tyranny which had arisen without their help; they could give it no other practical authority than what might flow from an imperial charter. The whole conduct of Charles in Italy was a scandalous political comedy. Matteo Villani relates how the Visconti escorted him round their territory, and at last out of it; how he went about like a hawker selling his wares (privileges, etc.) for money; what a mean appearance he made in Rome, and how at the end, without even drawing the sword, he returned with replenished coffers across the Alps. Sigismund came, on the first occasion at least (1414), with the good intention of persuading John XXIII to take part in his council; it was on that journey, when pope and emperor were gazing from the lofty tower of Cremona on the panorama of Lombardy, that their host, the tyrant Gabrino Fondolo, was seized with the desire to throw them both over. On his second visit Sigismund came as a mere adventurer; for more than half a year he remained shut up in Siena, like a debtor in gaol, and only with difficulty, and at a later period, succeeded in being crowned in Rome. And what can be thought of Frederick III? His journeys to Italy have the air of holiday-trips or pleasure-tours made at the expense of those who wanted him to confirm their prerogatives, or whose vanity it flattered to entertain an emperor. The latter was the case with Alfonso of Naples, who paid 150,000 florins for the honour of an imperial visit. At Ferrara, on his second return from Rome (1469), Frederick spent a whole day without leaving his chamber, distributing no less than eighty titles; he created knights, counts, doctors, notaries – counts, indeed, of different degrees, as, for instance, counts palatine, counts with the right to create doctors up to the number of five, counts with the right to legitimatize bastards, to appoint notaries, and so forth. The chancellor, however, expected in return for the patents in question a gratuity which was thought excessive at Ferrara. The opinion of Borso, himself created Duke of Modena and Reggio in return for an annual payment of 4,000 gold florins, when his imperial patron was distributing titles and diplomas to all the little court, is not mentioned. The humanists, then the chief spokesmen of the age, were divided in opinion according to their personal interests, while the emperor was greeted by some of them with the conventional acclamations of the poets of imperial Rome. Poggio confessed that he no longer knew what the coronation meant; in the old times only the victorious Imperator was crowned; and then he was crowned with laurel.

With Maximilian I begins not only the general intervention of foreign nations, but a new imperial policy with regard to Italy. The first step – the investiture of Lodovico il Moro with the duchy of Milan and the exclusion of his unhappy nephew – was not of a kind to bear good fruits. According to the modern theory of intervention, when two parties are tearing a country to pieces, a third may step in and take its share, and on this principle the empire acted. But right and justice were appealed to no longer. When Louis XII was expected in Genoa (1502), and the imperial eagle was removed from the hall of the ducal palace and replaced by painted lilies, the historian Senarega asked what, after all, was the meaning of the eagle which so many revolutions had spared, and what claims the empire had upon Genoa. No one knew more about the matter than the old phrase that Genoa was a *camera imperii*. In fact, nobody in Italy could give a clear answer to any such questions. At length, when Charles V held Spain and the empire together, he was able by means of Spanish forces to make good imperial claims; but it is notorious that what he thereby gained turned to the profit, not of the empire, but of the Spanish monarchy.

Closely connected with the political illegitimacy of the dynasties of the fifteenth century was the public indifference to legitimate birth, which to foreigners – for example, to Comines – appeared so remarkable. The two things went naturally together. In northern countries, as in Burgundy, the illegitimate offspring were provided for by a distinct class of appanages, such as bishoprics and the like; in Portugal an illegitimate line maintained itself on the throne only by constant effort; in Italy, on the contrary, there no longer existed a princely house where, even in the direct line of descent, bastards were not patiently tolerated. The Aragonese monarchs of Naples belonged to the illegitimate line, Aragon itself falling to the lot of the brother of Alfonso I. The great Frederick of Urbino was, perhaps, no Montefeltro at all. When Pius II was on his way to the Congress of Mantua (1459), eight bastards of the house of Este rode to meet him at Ferrara, among them the reigning duke Borso himself and two illegitimate sons of his illegitimate brother and predecessor Lionello. The latter had also had a lawful wife, herself an illegitimate daughter of Alfonso I of Naples by an African woman. The bastards were often admitted to the succession where the lawful children were minors and the dangers of the situation were pressing; and a rule of seniority became recognized, which took no account of pure of impure birth. The fitness of the individual, his worth and capacity, were of more weight than all the laws and usages which prevailed elsewhere in the West. It was the age, indeed, in which the sons of the popes were founding dynasties. In the sixteenth century, through the influence of foreign ideas and of the Counter-Reformation which then began, the whole question was judged more strictly: Varchi discovers that the succession of the legitimate children 'is ordered by reason, and is the will of heaven from eternity'. Cardinal Ippolito de' Medici founded his claim to the lordship of Florence on the fact that he was perhaps the fruit of a lawful marriage, and at all events son of a gentlewoman, and not, like Duke Alessandro, of a servant girl. At this time began those morganatic marriages of affection which in the fifteenth century, on grounds either of policy or morality, would have had no meaning at all.

But the highest and the most admired form of illegitimacy in the fifteenth century was presented by the *condottiere*, who, whatever may have been his origin, raised himself to the position of an independent ruler. At bottom, the occupation of Lower Italy by the Normans in the eleventh century was of this character. Such attempts now began to keep the peninsula in a constant ferment.

It was possible for a *condottiere* to obtain the lordship of a district even without usurpation, in the case when his employer, through want of money or troops, provided for him in this way; under any circumstances the *condottiere*, even when he dismissed for the time the greater part of his forces, needed a safe place where he could establish his winter quarters, and lay up his stores and provisions. The first example of a captain thus portioned is John Hawkwood, who was invested by Gregory XI with the lordship of Bagnacavallo and Cotignola. When with Alberigo de Barbiano Italian armies and leaders appeared upon the scene, the chances of founding a principality, or of increasing one already acquired, became more frequent. The first great bacchanalian outbreak of military ambition took place in the duchy of Milan after the death of Giangaleazzo (1402). The policy of his two sons was chiefly aimed at the destruction of the new despotisms founded by the *condottieri*; and from the greatest of them, Facino Cane, the house of Visconti inherited, together with his widow, a long list of cities, and 400,000 golden florins, not to speak of the soldiers of her first husband whom Beatrice di Tenda brought with her. From henceforth that thoroughly immoral relation between the governments and their *condottieri*, which is characteristic of the fifteenth century, became more and more common. An old story – one of those which are true and not true, everywhere and nowhere – describes it as follows: The citizens of a certain town (Siena seems to be meant) had once an officer in their service who had freed them from foreign aggression; daily they took counsel how to recompense him, and concluded that no reward in their power was great enough, not even if they made him lord of the city. At last one of them rose and said, 'Let us kill him and then worship him as our patron saint.' And so they did, following the example set by the Roman senate with Romulus. In fact, the *condottieri* had reason to fear none so much as their employers; if they were successful, they became dangerous, and were put out of the way like Roberto Malatesta just after the victory he had won for Sixtus IV (1482); if they failed, the vengeance of the Venetians on Carmagnola showed to what risks they were exposed (1432). It is characteristic of the moral aspect of the situation that the *condottieri* had often to give their wives and children as hostages, and notwithstanding this, neither felt nor inspired confidence. They must have been heroes of abnegation, natures like Belisarius himself, not to be cankered by hatred and bitterness; only the most perfect goodness could save them from the most monstrous iniquity. No wonder then if we find them full of contempt for all sacred things, cruel and treacherous to their fellows – men who cared nothing whether or no they died under the ban of the Church. At the same time, and through the force of the same conditions, the genius and capacity of many among them attained the highest conceivable development, and won for them the admiring devotion of their followers; their armies are the first in modern history in which the personal credit of the leader is the one moving power. A brilliant example is shown in the life of Francesco Sforza; no prejudice of birth could prevent him from winning and turning to account when he needed it a boundless devotion from each individual with whom he had to deal; it happened more than once that his enemies laid down their arms at the sight of him, greeting him reverently with uncovered heads, each honouring in him 'the common father of the men-at-arms'. The race of the Sforza has this special interest, that from the very beginning of its history we seem able to trace its endeavours after the crown. The foundation of its fortune lay in the remarkable fruitfulness of the family; Francesco's father, Jacopo, himself a celebrated man, had twenty brothers and sisters, all brought up roughly at Cotignola, near Faenza, amid the perils of one of the endless Romagnole vendettas between their own house and that of the Pasolini. The family dwelling was a mere arsenal and fortress; the mother and daughters were as warlike as their kinsmen. In his thirteenth year Jacopo ran away and fled to Panicale to the papal *condottiere* Boldrino – the man who even in death continued to lead his troops, the word of order being given from the bannered tent in which the embalmed body lay, till at last a fit leader was found to succeed him. Jacopo, when he had at length made himself a name in the service of different *condottieri*, sent for his relations, and obtained through them the same advantages that a prince derives from a numerous dynasty. It was these relations who kept the army together when he lay a captive in the Castel dell'Uovo at Naples; his sister took the royal envoys prisoner with her own hands, and saved him by this reprisal from death. It was an indication of the breadth and the range of his plans that in monetary affairs Jacopo was thoroughly trustworthy; even in his defeats he consequently found credit with the bankers. He habitually protected the peasants against the licence of his troops, and reluctantly destroyed or injured a conquered city. He gave his well-known mistress, Lucia, the mother of Francesco, in marriage to another, in order to be free for a princely alliance. Even the marriages of his relations were arranged on a definite plan. He kept clear of the impious and profligate life of his contemporaries, and brought up his son Francesco to the three rules: 'Let other men's wives alone; strike none of your followers, or, if you do, send the injured man far away; don't ride a hard-mouthed horse, or one that drops his shoe.' But his chief source of influence lay in the qualities, if not of a great general, at least of a great soldier. His frame was powerful, and developed by every kind of exercise; his peasant's face and frank manners won general popularity; his memory was marvellous, and after the lapse of years could recall the names of his followers, the number of their horses, and the amount of their pay. His education was purely Italian: he devoted his leisure to the study of history, and had Greek and Latin authors translated for his use. Francesco, his still more famous son, set his mind from the first on founding a powerful state, and through brilliant generalship and a faithlessness which hesitated at nothing, got possession of the great city of Milan (1447–50).

His example was contagious. Aeneas Sylvius wrote about this time: 'In our change-loving Italy, where nothing stands firm, and where no ancient dynasty exists, a servant can easily become a king.' One man in particular, who styles himself 'the man of fortune', filled the imagination of the whole country: Giacomo Piccinino, the son of Niccolò. It was a burning question of the day if he, too, would succeed in founding a princely house. The greater states had an obvious interest in hindering it, and even Francesco Sforza thought it would be all the better if the list of self-made sovereigns were not enlarged. But the troops and captains sent against him, at the time, for instance, when he was aiming at the lordship of Siena, recognized their interest in supporting him: 'If it were all over with him, we should have to go back and plough our fields.' Even while besieging him at Orbetello, they supplied him with provisions; and he got out of his straits with honour. But at last fate overtook him. All Italy was betting on the result, when (1465), after a visit to Sforza at Milan, he went to King Ferrante at Naples. In spite of the pledges given, and of his high connections, he was murdered in the Castel Nuovo. Even the *condottieri*, who had obtained their dominions by inheritance, never felt themselves safe. When Roberto Malatesta and Frederick of Urbino died on the same day (1482), the one at Rome, the other at Bologna, it was found that each had recommended his state to the care of the other. Against a class of men who themselves stuck at nothing, everything was held to be permissible. Francesco Sforza, when quite young, had married a rich Calabrian heiress, Polissena Russa, Countess of Montalto, who bore him a daughter; an aunt poisoned both mother and child, and seized the inheritance.

From the death of Piccinino onwards, the foundations of new states by the *condottieri* became a scandal not to be tolerated. The four great powers, Naples, Milan, the papacy and Venice, formed among themselves a political equilibrium which refused to allow of any disturbance. In the States of the Church, which swarmed with petty tyrants, who in part were, or had been, *condottieri*, the nephews of the popes, since the time of Sixtus IV, monopolized the right to all such undertakings. But at the first sign of a political crisis, the soldiers of fortune appeared again upon the scene. Under the wretched administration of Innocent VIII it was near happening that a certain Boccalino, who had formerly served in the Burgundian army, gave himself and the town of Osimo, of which he was master, up to the Turkish forces; fortunately, through the intervention of Lorenzo the Magnificent, he proved willing to be paid off, and took himself away. In the year 1495, when the wars of Charles VIII had turned Italy upside down, the *condottiere* Vidovero, of Brescia, made trial of his strength: he had already seized the town of Cesena and murdered many of the nobles and the burghers; but the citadel held out, and he was forced to withdraw. He then, at the head of a band lent him by another scoundrel, Pandolfo Malatesta of Rimini, son of the Roberto already spoken of, and Venetian *condottiere*, wrested the town of Castelnuovo from the Archbishop of Ravenna. The Venetians, fearing that worse would follow, and urged also by the pope, ordered Pandolfo, 'with the kindest intentions', to take an opportunity of arresting his good friend: the arrest was made, though 'with great regret', whereupon the order came to bring the prisoner to the gallows. Pandolfo was considerate enough to strangle him in prison, and then show his corpse to the people. The last notable example of such usurpers is the famous castellan of Musso, who, during the confusion in the Milanese territory which followed the battle of Pavia (1525), improvised a sovereignty on the Lake of Como.

The Smaller Despotisms

It may be said in general of the despotisms of the fifteenth century that the greatest crimes are most frequent in the smallest states. In these, where the family was numerous and all the members wished to live in a manner befitting their rank, disputes respecting the inheritance were unavoidable. Bernardo Varano of Camerino put two of his brothers to death (1434), wishing to divide their property among his sons. Where the ruler of a single town was distinguished by a wise, moderate and humane government, and by zeal for intellectual culture, he was generally a member of some great family, or politically dependent on it. This was the case, for example, with Alessandro Sforza, Prince of Pesaro (d. 1473), brother of the great Francesco, and step-father of Frederick of Urbino. Prudent in administration, just and affable in his rule, he enjoyed, after years of warfare, a tranquil reign, collected a noble library, and passed his leisure in learned or religious conversation. A man of the same class was Giovanni II Bentivoglio of Bologna (1462–1506), whose policy was determined by that of the Este and the Sforza. What ferocity and bloodthirstiness is found, on the other hand, among the Varani of Camerino, the Malatesta of Rimini, the Manfreddi of Faenza, and above all among the Baglioni of Perugia. We find a striking picture of the events in the last-named family, towards the close of the fifteenth century, in the admirable historical narratives of Graziani and Matarazzo.

The Baglioni were one of those families whose rule never took the shape of an avowed despotism. It was rather a leadership exercised by means of their vast wealth and of their practical influence in the choice of public officers. Within the family one man was recognized as head; but deep and secret jealousy prevailed among the members of the different branches. Opposed to the Baglioni stood another aristocratic party, led by the family of the Oddi. In 1487 the city was turned into a camp, and the houses of the leading citizens swarmed with bravos; scenes of violence were of daily occurrence. At the burial of a German student, who had been assassinated, two colleges took arms against one another; sometimes the bravos of the different houses even joined battle in the public square. The complaints of the merchants and artisans were vain; the papal governors and *nipoti* held their tongues, or took themselves off on the first opportunity. At last the Oddi were forced to abandon Perugia, and the city became a beleaguered fortress under the absolute despotism of the Baglioni, who used even the cathedral as barracks. Plots and surprises were met with cruel vengeance; in the year 1491, after 130 conspirators who had forced their way into the city were killed and hung up at the Palazzo Comunale, thirty-five altars were erected in the square, and for three days mass was performed and processions held, to take away the curse which rested on the spot. A nephew of Innocent VIII was in open day run through in the street. A nephew of Alexander VI, who was sent to smooth matters over, was dismissed with public contempt. All the while the two leaders of the ruling house, Guido and Ridolfo, were holding frequent interviews with Suor Colomba of Rieti, a Dominican nun of saintly reputation and miraculous powers, who under penalty of some great disaster ordered them to make peace – naturally in vain. Nevertheless the chronicle takes the opportunity to point out the devotion and piety of the better men in Perugia during this reign of terror. When in 1494 Charles VIII approached, the Baglioni from Perugia and the exiles encamped in and near Assisi conducted the war with such ferocity that every house in the valley was levelled to the ground. The fields lay untilled, the peasants were turned into plundering and murdering savages, the fresh-grown bushes were filled with stags and wolves, and the beasts grew fat on the bodies of the slain, on so-called 'Christian flesh'. When Alexander VI withdrew (1495) into Umbria before Charles VIII, then returning from Naples, it occurred to him, when at Perugia, that he might now rid himself of the Baglioni once for all; he proposed to Guido a festival or tournament, or something else of the same kind, which would bring the whole family together. Guido, however, was of the opinion 'that the most impressive spectacle of all would be to see the whole military force of Perugia collected in a body', whereupon the pope abandoned his project. Soon after, the exiles made another attack in which nothing but the personal heroism of the Baglioni won them the victory. It was then that Simonetto Baglione, a lad of scarcely eighteen, fought in the square with a handful of followers against hundreds of the enemy: he fell at last with more than twenty wounds, but recovered himself when Astorre Baglione came to his help, and mounting on horseback in gilded armour with a falcon on his helmet, 'like Mars in bearing and in deeds, plunged into the struggle'.

At that time Raphael, a boy of twelve years of age, was at school under Pietro Perugino. The impressions of these days are perhaps immortalized in the small, early pictures of St Michael and St George: something of them, it may be, lives eternally in the great painting of St Michael: and if Astorre Baglione has anywhere found his apotheosis, it is in the figure of the heavenly horseman in the Heliodorus.

The opponents of the Baglioni were partly destroyed, partly scattered in terror, and were henceforth incapable of another enterprise of the kind. After a time a partial reconciliation took place, and some of the exiles were allowed to return. But Perugia became none the safer or more tranquil: the inward discord of the ruling family broke out in frightful excesses. An opposition was formed against Guido and Ridolfo and their sons Gianpaolo, Simonetto, Astorre, Gismondo, Gentile, Marcantinio and others, by two great-nephews, Grifone and Carlo Barciglia; the latter of the two was also nephew of Varano, Prince of Camerino, and brother-in-law of one of the former exiles, Ieronimo della Penna. In vain did Simonetto, warned by sinister presentiment, entreat his uncle on his knees to allow him to put Penna to death: Guido refused. The plot ripened suddenly on the occasion of the marriage of Astorre with Lavinia Colonna, at midsummer 1500. The festival began and lasted several days amid gloomy forebodings, whose deepening effect is admirably described by Matarazzo. Varano fed and encouraged them with devilish ingenuity: he worked upon Grifone by the prospect of undivided authority, and by stories of an imaginary intrigue of his wife Zenobia with Gianpaolo. Finally each conspirator was provided with a victim. (The Baglioni lived all of them in separate houses, mostly on the site of the present castle.) Each received fifteen of the bravos at hand; the remainder were set on the watch. In the night of 15 July the doors were forced, and Guido, Astorre, Simonetto and Gismondo were murdered; the others succeeded in escaping.

As the corpse of Astorre lay by that of Simonetto in the street, the spectators, 'and especially the foreign students', compared him to an ancient Roman, so great and imposing did he seem. In the features of Simonetto could still be traced the audacity and defiance which death itself had not tamed. The victors went round among the friends of the family, and did their best to recommend themselves; they found all in tears and preparing to leave for the country. Meantime the escaped Baglioni collected forces without the city, and on the following day forced their way in, Gianpaolo at their head, and speedily found adherents among others whom Barciglia had been threatening with death. When Grifone fell into their hands near Sant' Ercolano, Gianpaolo handed him over for execution to his followers. Barciglia and Penna fled to Varano, the chief author of the tragedy, at Camerino; and in a moment, almost without loss, Gianpaolo became master of the city.

Atalanta, the still young and beautiful mother of Grifone, who the day before had withdrawn to a country house with the latter's wife Zenobia and two children of

Gianpaolo, and more than once had repulsed her son with a mother's curse, now returned with her daughter-in-law in search of the dying man. All stood aside as the two women approached, each man shrinking from being recognized as the slayer of Grifone, and dreading the malediction of the mother. But they were deceived: she herself besought her son to pardon him who had dealt the fatal blow, and he died with her blessing. The eyes of the crowd followed the two women reverently as they crossed the square with blood-stained garments. It was Atalanta for whom Raphael afterwards painted the world-famed *Deposition*, with which she laid her own maternal sorrows at the feet of a yet higher and holier suffering.

The cathedral, in the immediate neighbourhood of which the greater part of this tragedy had been enacted, was washed with wine and consecrated afresh. The triumphal arch, erected for the wedding, still remained standing, painted with the deeds of Astorre and with the laudatory verses of the narrator of these events, the worthy Matarazzo.

A legendary history, which is simply the reflection of these atrocities, arose out of the early days of the Baglioni. All the members of this family from the beginning were reported to have died an evil death – twenty-seven on one occasion together; their houses were said to have been once before levelled to the ground, and the streets of Perugia paved with the bricks – and more of the same kind. Under Paul III the destruction of their palaces really took place.

For a time they seemed to have formed good resolutions, to have brought their own party into order, and to have protected the public officials against the arbitrary acts of the nobility. But the old curse broke out again like a smouldering fire. In 1520 Gianpaolo was enticed to Rome under Leo X, and there beheaded; one of his sons, Orazio, who ruled in Perugia for a short time only, and by the most violent means, as the partisan of the Duke of Urbino (himself threatened by the pope), once more repeated in his own family the horrors of the past. His uncle and three cousins were murdered, whereupon the duke sent him word that enough had been done. His brother, Malatesta Baglione, the Florentine general, has made himself immortal by the treason of 1530; and Malatesta's son Ridolfo, the last of the house, attained, by the murder of the legate and the public officers in the year 1534, a brief but sanguinary authority.

Here and there we meet with the names of the rulers of Rimini. Unscrupulousness, impiety, military skill and high culture have been seldom combined in one individual as in Sigismondo Malatesta (d. 1467). But the accumulated crimes of such a family must at last outweigh all talent, however great, and drag the tyrant into the abyss. Pandolfo, Sigismondo's nephew, who has been mentioned already, succeeded in holding his ground, for the sole reason that the Venetians refused to abandon their *condottiere*, whatever guilt he might be chargeable with; when his subjects, after ample provocation, bombarded him in his castle at Rimini (1497), and afterwards allowed him to escape, a Venetian commissioner brought him back, stained as he was with fratricide and every other abomination. Thirty years later the Malatesta were penniless exiles. In the year 1527, as in the time of Cesare Borgia, a sort of epidemic fell on the petty tyrants; few of them outlived this date, and none to their own good. At Mirandola, which was governed by insignificant princes of the house of Pico, lived in the year 1533 a poor scholar, Lilio Gregorio Giraldi, who had fled from the sack of Rome to the hospitable hearth of the aged Giovanni Francesco Pico, nephew of the famous Giovanni; the discussions as to the sepulchral monument which the prince was constructing for himself gave rise to a treatise, the dedication of which bears the date of April in this year. The postscript is a sad one – 'In October of the same year the unhappy prince was attacked in the night and robbed of life and throne by his brother's son; and I myself escaped narrowly, and am now in the deepest misery.'

A pseudo-despotism without characteristic features, such as Pandolfo Petrucci exercised from the year 1490 in Siena, then torn by faction, is hardly worth a closer consideration. Insignificant and malicious, he governed with the help of a professor of jurisprudence and of an astrologer, and frightened his people by an occasional murder. His pastime in the summer months was to roll blocks of stone from the top of Monte Amiata, without caring what or whom they hit. After succeeding, where the most prudent failed, in escaping from the devices of Cesare Borgia, he died at last forsaken and despised. His sons maintained a qualified supremacy for many years afterwards.

The Greater Dynasties

In treating of the chief dynasties of Italy, it is convenient to discuss the Aragonese, on account of its special character, apart from the rest. The feudal system, which from the days of the Normans had survived in the form of a territorial supremacy of the barons, gave a distinctive colour to the political constitution of Naples; while elsewhere in Italy, excepting only in the southern part of the ecclesiastical dominion, and in a few other districts, a direct tenure of land prevailed, and no hereditary powers were permitted by the law. The great Alfonso, who reigned in Naples from 1435 onwards (d. 1458), was a man of another kind than his real or alleged descendants. Brilliant in his whole existence, fearless in mixing with his people, dignified and affable in intercourse, admired rather than blamed even for his old man's passion for Lucrezia d'Alagnam, he had the one bad quality of extravagance, from which, however, the natural consequence followed. Unscrupulous financiers were long omnipotent at court, till the bankrupt king robbed them of their spoils; a crusade was preached as a pretext for taxing the clergy; when a great earthquake happened in the Abruzzi, the survivors were compelled to make good the contributions of the dead. By such means Alfonso was able to entertain distinguished guests with unrivalled splendour; he found pleasure in ceaseless expense, even for the benefit of his enemies, and in rewarding literary work knew absolutely no measure. Poggio received 500 pieces of gold for translating Xenophon's *Cyropaedeia*.

Ferrante, who succeeded him, passed as his illegitimate son by a Spanish lady, but was not improbably the son of a half-caste Moor of Valencia. Whether it was his blood or the plots formed against his life by the barons which embittered and darkened his nature, it is certain that he was equalled in ferocity by none among the princes of his time. Restlessly active, recognized as one of the most powerful political minds of the day, and free from the vices of the profligate, he concentrated all his powers, among which must be reckoned profound dissimulation and an irreconcilable spirit of vengeance, on the destruction of his opponents. He had been wounded in every point in which a ruler is open to offence; for the leaders of the barons, though related to him by marriage, were yet the allies of his foreign enemies. Extreme measures became part of his daily policy. The means for this struggle with his barons, and for his external wars, were exacted in the same Muhammadan fashion which Frederick II had introduced: the government alone dealt in oil and corn; the whole commerce of the country was put by Ferrante into the hands of a wealthy merchant, Francesco Coppola, who had entire control of the anchorage on the coast, and shared the profits with the king. Deficits were made up by forced loans, by executions and confiscations, by open simony, and by contributions levied on the ecclesiastical corporations. Besides hunting, which he practised regardless of all rights of property, his pleasures were of two kinds: he liked to have his opponents near him, either alive in well-guarded prisons, or dead and embalmed, dressed in the costume which they wore in their lifetime. He would chuckle in talking of the captives with his friends, and made no secret whatever of the museum of mummies. His victims were mostly men whom he had got into his power by treachery; some were even seized while guests at the royal table. His conduct to his first minister, Antolello Petrucci, who had grown sick and grey in his service, and from whose increasing fear of death he extorted 'present after present', was literally devilish. At length the suspicion of complicity with the last conspiracy of the barons gave the pretext for his arrest and execution. With him died Coppola. The way in which all this is narrated in Caracciolo and Porzio makes one's hair stand on end.

The elder of the king's sons, Alfonso, Duke of Calabria, enjoyed in later years a kind of co-regency with his father. He was a savage, brutal profligate, who in point of frankness alone had the advantage of Ferrante, and who openly avowed his contempt for religion and its usages. The better and nobler features of the Italian despotisms are not to be found among the princes of this line; all that they possessed of the art and culture of their time served the purposes of luxury or display. Even the genuine Spaniards seem to have almost always degenerated in Italy; but the end of this cross-bred house (1494 and 1503) gives clear proof of a want of blood. Ferrante died of mental care and trouble; Alfonso accused his brother Federigo, the only honest member of the family, of treason, and insulted him in the vilest manner. At length, though he had hitherto passed for one of the ablest generals in Italy, he lost his head and fled to Sicily, leaving his son, the younger

Ferrante, a prey to the French and to domestic treason. A dynasty which had ruled as this had done must at least have sold its life dear, if its children were ever to hope for a restoration. But, as Comines one-sidedly and yet on the whole rightly observes on this occasion, '*Jamais homme cruel ne fut plus hardi*': there was never a more cruel man.

The despotism of the dukes of Milan, whose government from the time of Giangaleazzo onwards was an absolute monarchy of the most thoroughgoing sort, shows the genuine Italian character of the fifteenth century. The last of the Visconti, Filippo Maria (1412–47), is a character of peculiar interest, and of which fortunately an admirable description has been left us. What a man of uncommon gifts and high position can be made by the passion of fear is here shown with what may be called a mathematical completeness. All the resources of the state were devoted to the one end of securing his personal safety, though happily his cruel egotism did not degenerate into a purposeless thirst for blood. He lived in the Citadel of Milan, surrounded by magnificent gardens, arbours and lawns. For years he never set foot in the city, making his excursions only in the country, where lay several of his splendid castles; the flotilla which, drawn by the swiftest horses, conducted him to them along canals constructed for the purpose, was so arranged as to allow of the application of the most rigorous etiquette. Whoever entered the Citadel was watched by a hundred eyes; it was forbidden even to stand at the window, lest signs should be given to those without. All who were admitted among the personal followers of the prince were subjected to a series of the strictest examinations; then, once accepted, were charged with the highest diplomatic commissions, as well as with the humblest personal services – both in this court being alike honourable. And this was the man who conducted long and difficult wars, who dealt habitually with political affairs of the first importance, and every day sent his plenipotentiaries to all parts of Italy. His safety lay in the fact that none of his servants trusted the others, that his *condottieri* were watched and misled by spies, and that the ambassadors and higher officials were baffled and kept apart by artificially nourished jealousies, and in particular by the device of coupling an honest man with a knave. His inward faith, too, rested upon opposed and contradictory systems; he believed in blind necessity, and in the influence of the stars, and offering prayers at one and the same time to helpers of every sort; he was a student of the ancient authors, as well as of French tales of chivalry. And yet the same man, who would never suffer death to be mentioned in his presence, and caused his dying favourites to be removed from the castle, that no shadow might fall on the abode of happiness, deliberately hastened his own death by closing up a wound, and, refusing to be bled, died at last with dignity and grace.

His son-in-law and successor, the fortunate *condottiere* Francesco Sforza (1450–66), was perhaps of all the Italians of the fifteenth century the man most after the heart of his age. Never was the triumph of genius and individual power more brilliantly displayed than in him; and those who would not recognize his merit were at least forced to wonder at him as the spoilt child of fortune. The Milanese claimed it openly as an honour to be governed by so distinguished a master; when he entered the city the thronging populace bore him on horseback into the cathedral, without giving him the chance to dismount. Let us listen to the balance-sheet of his life, in the estimate of Pope Pius II, a judge in such matters:

> In the year 1459, when the duke came to the congress at Mantua, he was sixty (really fifty-eight) years old; on horseback he looked like a young man; of a lofty and imposing figure, with serious features, calm and affable in conversation, princely in his whole bearing, with a combination of bodily and intellectual gifts unrivalled in our time, unconquered on the field of battle – such was the man who raised himself from a humble position to the control of an empire. His wife was beautiful and virtuous, his children were like the angels of heaven; he was seldom ill, and all his chief wishes were fulfilled. And yet he was not without misfortune. His wife, out of jealousy, killed his mistress; his old comrades and friends, Troilo and Brunoro, abandoned him and went over to King Alfonso; another, Ciarpollone, he was forced to hang for treason; he had to suffer it that his brother Alessandro set the French upon him; one of his sons formed intrigues against him, and was imprisoned; the March of Ancona, which he had won in war, he lost again the same way. No man enjoys so unclouded a fortune, that he has not somewhere to struggle with adversity. He is happy who has but few troubles.

With this negative definition of happiness the learned pope dismisses the reader. Had he been able to see into the future, or been willing to stop and discuss the consequences of an uncontrolled despotism, one pervading fact would not have escaped his notice – the absence of all guarantee for the future. Those children, beautiful as angels, carefully and thoroughly educated as they were, fell victims, when they grew up, to the corruption of a measureless egotism. Galeazzo Maria (1466–76), solicitous only of outward effect, took pride in the beauty of his hands, in the high salaries he paid, in the financial credit he enjoyed, in his treasure of two million pieces of gold, in the distinguished people who surrounded him, and in the army and birds of chase which he maintained. He was fond of the sound of his own voice, and spoke well, most fluently, perhaps, when he had the chance of insulting a Venetian ambassador. He was subject to caprices, such as having a room painted with figures in a single night; and, what was worse, to fits of senseless debauchery and of revolting cruelty to his nearest friends. To a handful of enthusiasts, he seemed a tyrant too bad to live; they murdered him, and thereby delivered the state into the power of his brothers, one of whom, Lodovico il Moro, threw his nephew into prison, and took the government into his own hands. From this usurpation followed the French intervention, and the disasters which befell the whole of Italy.

Lodovico Sforza, called 'il Moro', the Moor, is the most perfect type of the despot of that age, and, as a kind of natural product, almost disarms our moral judgement. Notwithstanding the profound immorality of the means he employed, he used them with perfect ingeniousness; no one would probably have been more astonished than himself to learn that for the choice of means as well as of ends a human being is morally responsible; he would rather have reckoned it as a singular virtue that, so far as possible, he had abstained from too free a use of the punishment of death. He accepted as no more than his due the almost fabulous respect of the Italians for his political genius. In 1496 he boasted that the Pope Alexander was his chaplain, the Emperor Maximilian his *condottiere*, Venice his chamberlain, and the King of France his courier, who must come and go at his bidding. With marvellous presence of mind he weighed, even in his last extremity (1499), all possible means of escape, and at length decided, to his honour, to trust to the goodness of human nature; he rejected the proposal of his brother, the Cardinal Ascanio, who wished to remain in the Citadel of Milan, on the ground of a former quarrel: 'Monsignore, take it not ill, but I trust you not, brother though you be'; and appointed to the command of the castle, 'that pledge of his return', a man to whom he had always done good, but who nevertheless betrayed him. At home the Moor was a good and useful ruler, and to the last he reckoned on his popularity both in Milan and in Como. In later years (after 1496) he had overstrained the resources of his state, and at Cremona had ordered, out of pure expediency, a respectable citizen, who had spoken against the new taxes, to be quietly strangled. Since that time, in holding audiences, he kept his visitors away from his person by means of a bar, so that in conversing with him they were compelled to speak at the top of their voices. At his court, the most brilliant in Europe, since that of Burgundy had ceased to exist, immorality of the worst kind was prevalent; the daughter was sold by the father, the wife by the husband, the sister by the brother. The prince himself was incessantly active, and, as son of his own deeds, claimed relationship with all who, like himself, stood on their personal merits – with scholars, poets, artists and musicians. The academy which he founded served rather for his own purposes than for the instruction of scholars; nor was it the fame of the distinguished men who surrounded him which he heeded, so much as their society and their services. It is certain that Bramante was scantily paid at first; Leonardo, on the other hand, was up to 1496 suitably remunerated – and besides, what kept him at the court, if not his own free will? The world lay open to him, as perhaps to no other mortal man of that day; and if proof were wanting of the loftier element in the nature of Lodovico il Moro, it is found in the long stay of the enigmatic master at his court. That afterwards Leonardo entered the service of Cesare Borgia and Francis I was probably due to the interest he felt in the unusual and striking character of the two men.

After the fall of the Moor, his sons were badly brought up among strangers. The elder, Massimiliano, had no resemblance to him; the younger, Francesco, was at all events not without spirit. Milan, which in those years changed its rulers so often, and suffered so unspeakably in the change, endeavored to secure itself against a reaction. In the year 1512 the French, retreating before the arms of Maximilian and the Spaniards, were induced to make a declaration that the Milanese had taken no part in their expulsion, and, without being guilty of rebellion, might yield themselves to a new conqueror. It is a fact of some political importance that in such moments of transition the unhappy city, like Naples at the flight of the Aragonese, was apt to fall a prey to gangs of (often highly aristocratic) scoundrels.

The house of Gonzaga at Mantua and that of Montefeltro of Urbino were among the best ordered and richest in men of ability during the second half of the fifteenth century. The Gonzaga were a tolerably harmonious family; for a long period no murder had been known among them, and their dead could be shown to the world without fear. The Marquis Francesco Gonzaga and his wife, Isabella of Este, in spite of some few irregularities, were a united and respectable couple, and brought up their sons to be successful and remarkable men at a time when their small but most important state was exposed to incessant danger. That Francesco, either as statesman or as soldier, should adopt a policy of exceptional honesty, was what neither the emperor, nor Venice, nor the King of France could have expected or desired; but certainly since the battle of the Taro (1495), so far as military honour was concerned, he felt and acted as an Italian patriot, and imparted the same spirit to his wife. Every deed of loyalty and heroism, such as the defence of Faenza against Cesare Borgia, she felt as a vindication of the honour of Italy. Our judgement of her does not need to rest on the praises of the artists and writers who made the fair princess a rich return for her patronage; her own letters show her to us as a woman of unshaken firmness, full of kindliness and humorous observation. Bembo, Bandello, Ariosto and Bernardo Tasso sent their works to this court, small and powerless as it was, and empty as they found its treasury. A more polished and charming circle was not to be seen in Italy, since the dissolution (1508) of the old court of Urbino; and in one respect, in freedom of movement, the society of Ferrara was inferior to that of Mantua. In artistic matters Isabella had an accurate knowledge, and the catalogue of her small but choice collection can be read by no lover of art without emotion.

In the great Federigo (1444–82), whether he were a genuine Montefeltro or not, Urbino possessed a brilliant representative of the princely order. As a *condottiere* he shared the political morality of soldiers of fortune, a morality of which the fault does not rest with them alone; as ruler of his little territory he adopted the plan of spending at home the money he had earned abroad, and taxing his people as lightly as possible. Of him and his two successors, Guidobaldo and Francesco Maria, we read: 'They erected buildings, furthered the cultivation of the land, lived at home, and gave employment to a large number of people: their subjects loved them.' But not only the state, but the court too, was a work of art and organization, and this in every sense of the word. Federigo had 500 persons in his service; the arrangements of the court were as complete as in the capitals of the greatest monarchs, but nothing was wasted; all had its object, and all was carefully watched and controlled. The court was no scene of vice and dissipation: it served as a school of military education for the sons of other great houses, the thoroughness of whose culture and instruction was made a point of honour by the duke. The palace which he built, if not one of the most splendid, was classical in the perfection of its plan; there was placed the greatest of his treasures, the celebrated library. Feeling secure in a land where all gained profit or employment from his rule, and where none were beggars, he habitually went about unarmed and almost unaccompanied; alone among the princes of his time he ventured to walk in an open park, and to take his frugal meals in an open chamber, while Livy, or in time of fasting some devotional work, was read to him. In the course of the same afternoon he would listen to a lecture on some classical subject, and thence would go to the monastery of the Clarisses and talk of sacred things through the grating with the abbess. In the evening he would overlook the martial exercises of the young people of his court on the meadow of San Francesco, known for its magnificent view, and saw to it well that all the feats were done in the most perfect manner. He strove always to be affable and accessible to the utmost degree, visiting the artisans who worked for him in their shops, holding frequent audiences, and, if possible, attending to the requests of each individual on the same day that they were presented. No wonder that the people, as he walked along the street, knelt down and cried: '*Dio ti mantenga, signore!*' He was called by thinking people 'the light of Italy'. His gifted son Guidobaldo, visited by sickness and misfortune of every kind, was able at the last (1508) to give his state into the safe hands of his nephew Francesco Maria (nephew also of Pope Julius II), who at least succeeded in preserving the territory from any permanent foreign occupation. It is remarkable with what confidence Guidobaldo yielded and fled before Cesare Borgia and Francesco before the troops of Leo X; each knew that his restoration would be all the easier and the more popular the less the country suffered through a fruitless defence. When Lodo-vico made the same calculation at Milan, he forgot the many grounds of hatred which existed against him. The court of Guidobaldo has been made immortal as the high school of polished manners by Baldassare Castiglione, who represented his eclogue 'Thyrsis' before, and in honour of, that society (1506), and who afterwards (1518) laid the scene of the dialogue of his *Cortigiano* in the circle of the accomplished Duchess Elisabetta Gonzaga.

The government of the family of Este at Ferrara, Modena and Reggio displays curious contrasts of violence and popularity. Within the palace frightful deeds were perpetrated; a princess was beheaded (1425) for alleged adultery with a step-son; legitimate and illegitimate children fled from the court, and even abroad their lives were threatened by assassins sent in pursuit of them (1471). Plots from without were incessant; the bastard of a bastard tried to wrest the crown from the lawful heir, Ercole I; this latter is said afterwards (1493) to have poisoned his wife on discovering that she, at the instigation of her brother Ferrante of Naples, was going to poison him. This list of tragedies is closed by the plot of two bastards against their brothers, the ruling Duke Alfonso I and Cardinal Ippolito (1506), which was discovered in time, and punished with imprisonment for life. The financial system in this state was of the most perfect kind, and necessarily so, since none of the large or second-rate powers of Italy were exposed to such danger and stood in such constant need of armaments and fortifications. It was the hope of the rulers that the increasing prosperity of the people would keep pace with the increasing weight of taxation, and the Marquis Niccolò (d. 1441) used to express the wish that his subjects might be richer than the people of other countries. If the rapid increase of the population be a measure of prosperity actually attained, it is certainly a fact of importance that in the year 1497, notwithstanding the wonderful extension of the capital, no houses were to be let. Ferrara is the first really modern city in Europe; large and well-built quarters sprang up at the bidding of the ruler: here, by the concentration of the official classes and the active promotion of trade, was formed for the first time a true capital; wealthy fugitives from all parts of Italy, Florentines especially, settled and built their palaces at Ferrara. But the indirect taxation, at all events, must have reached a point at which it could only just be borne. The government, it is true, took measures of alleviation which were also adopted by other Italian despots, such as Galeazzo Maria Sforza: in time of famine corn was brought from a distance and seems to have been distributed gratuitously; but in ordinary times it compensated itself by the monopoly, if not of corn, of many other of the necessaries of life – fish, salt, meat, fruit and vegetables, which last were carefully planted on and near the walls of the city. The most considerable source of income, however, was the annual sale of public offices, a usage which was common throughout Italy, and about the working of which at Ferrara we have more precise information. We read, for example, that at the new year 1502 the majority of the officials bought their places at '*prezzi salati*'; public servants of the most various kinds, custom-house officers, bailiffs (*massari*), notaries, '*podestà*', judges and even captains, i.e. lieutenant-governors of provincial towns, are quoted by name. As one of the 'devourers of the people' who paid dearly for their places, and who were 'hated worse than the devil', Tito Strozza – let us hope not the famous Latin poet – is mentioned. About the same time every year the dukes were accustomed to make a round of visits in Ferrara, the so-called '*andar per ventura*', in which they took presents from, at any rate, the more wealthy citizens. The gifts, however, did not consist of money, but of natural products.

It was the pride of the duke for all Italy to know that at Ferrara the soldiers received their pay and the professors at the university their salary not a day later than it was due; that the soldiers never dared lay arbitrary hands on a citizen or peasant; that the town was impregnable to assault; and that vast sums of coined money were stored up in the citadel. To keep two sets of accounts seemed unnecessary: the Minister of Finance was at the same time manager of the ducal household. The buildings erected by Borso (1430–71), by Ercole I (till 1505), and by Alfonso I (till 1534), were very numerous, but of small size; they are characteristic of a princely house which, with all its love of splendour – Borso never appeared but in embroidery and jewels – indulged in no ill-considered expense. Alfonso may perhaps have foreseen the fate which was in store for his charming little villas, the Belvedere with its shady gardens, and Montana with its fountains and beautiful frescoes.

It is undeniable that the dangers to which these princes were constantly exposed developed in them capacities of a remarkable kind. In so artificial a world only a man of consummate address could hope to succeed; each candidate for distinction was forced to make good his claims by personal merit and show himself worthy of the crown he sought. Their characters are not without dark sides; but in all of them lives something of those qualities which Italy then pursued as its ideal. What European monarch of the time laboured for his own culture as, for instance, Alfonso I? His travels in France, England and the Netherlands were undertaken for the purpose of study: by means of them he gained an accurate knowledge of the industry and commerce of these countries. It is ridiculous to reproach him with the turner's work which he practised in his leisure hours, connected as it was with his skill in the casting of cannon, and with the unprejudiced freedom with which he surrounded himself by masters of every art. The Italian princes were not, like their contemporaries in the North, dependent on the society of an aristocracy which held itself to be the only class worth consideration, and which infected the monarch with the same conceit. In Italy the prince was permitted and compelled to know and to use men of every grade in society; and the nobility, though by birth a caste, were forced in social intercourse to stand upon their personal qualifications alone. But this is a point which we shall discuss more fully in the sequel.

The feeling of the Ferrarese towards the ruling house was a strange compound of silent dread, of the truly Italian sense of well-calculated interest, and of the loyalty of the modern subject: personal admiration was transferred into a new sentiment of duty. The city of Ferrara raised in 1451 a bronze equestrian statue to their Prince Niccolò, who had died ten years earlier; Borso (1454) did not scruple to place his own statue, also of bronze, but in a sitting posture, hard by in the market; in addition to which the city, at the beginning of his reign, decreed to him a 'marble triumphal pillar'. A citizen who, when abroad in Venice, had spoken ill of Borso in public was informed against on his return home, and condemned to banishment and the confiscation of his goods; a loyal subject was with difficulty restrained from cutting him down before the tribunal itself, and with a rope round his neck the offender went to the duke and begged for a full pardon. The government was well provided with spies, and the duke inspected personally the daily list of travellers which the inn-keepers were strictly ordered to present. Under Borso, who was anxious to leave no distinguished stranger unhonoured, this regulation served a hospitable purpose; Ercole I used it simply as a measure of precaution. In Bologna, too, it was then the rule, under Giovanni II Bentivoglio, that every passing traveller who entered at one gate must obtain a ticket in order to go out at another. An unfailing means of popularity was the sudden dismissal of oppressive officials. When Borso arrested in person his chief and confidential counsellors, when Ercole I removed and disgraced a tax-gatherer who for years had been sucking the blood of the people, bonfires were lighted and the bells were pealed in their honour. With one of his servants, however, Ercole let things go too far. The director of the police, or by whatever name we should choose to call him (*capitano di giustizia*), was Gregorio Zampante of Lucca – a native being unsuited for an office of this kind. Even the sons and brothers of the duke trembled before this man; the fines he inflicted amounted to hundreds and thousands of ducats, and torture was applied even before the hearing of a case: bribes were accepted from wealthy criminals, and their pardon obtained from the duke by false representations. Gladly would the people have paid any sum to this ruler for sending away the 'enemy of God and man'. But Ercole had knighted him and made him godfather to his children; and year by year Zampante laid by 2,000 ducats. He dared only eat pigeons bred in his own house, and could not cross the street without a band of archers and bravos. It was time to get rid of him; in 1496 two students and a converted Jew whom he had mortally offended killed him in his house while he was taking his siesta, and then rode through the town on horses held in waiting, raising the cry, 'Come out! Come out! We have slain Zampante!' The pursuers came too late, and found them already safe across the frontier. Of course it now rained satires – some of them in the form of sonnets, others of odes.

It was wholly in the spirit of this system that the sovereign imposed his own respect for useful servants on the court and on the people. When in 1469 Borso's privy councillor Lodovico Casella died, no court of law or place of business in the city, and no lecture-room at the university, was allowed to be open: all had to follow the body to San Domenico, since the duke intended to be present. And, in fact, 'the first of the house of Este who attended the corpse of a subject' walked, clad in black, after the coffin, weeping, while behind him came the relatives of Casella, each conducted by one of the gentlemen of the court: the body of the plain citizen was carried by nobles from the church into the cloister, where it was buried.

Indeed this official sympathy with princely emotion first came up in the Italian states. At the root of the practice may be a beautiful, humane sentiment; the utterance of it, especially in the poets, is, as a rule, of equivocal sincerity. One of the youthful poems of Ariosto, on the death of Leonora of Aragon, wife of Ercole I, contains besides the inevitable graveyard flowers, which are scattered in the elegies of all ages, some thoroughly modern features:

> This death had given Ferrara a blow which it would not get over for years: its benefactress was now its advocate in heaven, since earth was not worthy of her; truly the angel of Death did not come to her, as to us common mortals, with blood-stained scythe, but fair to behold [*onesta*] and with so kind a face that every fear was allayed.

But we meet, also, with a sympathy of a different kind. Novelists, depending wholly on the favour of their patrons, tell us the love-stories of the prince, even before his death, in a way which, to later times, would seem the height of indiscretion, but which then passed simply as an innocent compliment. Lyrical poets even went so far as to sing the illicit flames of their lawfully married lords, e.g. Angelo Poliziano, those of Lorenzo the Magnificent, and Gioviano Pontano, with a singular gusto, those of Alfonso of Calabria. The poem in question betrays unconsciously the odious disposition of the Aragonese ruler; in these things too, he must needs be the most fortunate, else woe be to those who are more successful! That the greatest artists, for example Leonardo, should paint the mistresses of their patrons was no more than a matter of course.

But the house of Este was not satisfied with the praises of others; it undertook to celebrate them itself. In the Palazzo Schifanoia Borso caused himself to be painted in a series of historical representations, and Ercole (from 1472 on) kept the anniversary of his accession to the throne by a procession which was compared to the feast of Corpus Christi; shops were closed as on Sunday; in the centre of the line walked all the members of the princely house (bastards included) clad in embroidered robes. That the crown was the fountain of honour and authority, that all personal distinction flowed from it alone, had been long expressed at this court by the Order of the Golden Spur – an order which had nothing in common with medieval chivalry. Ercole I added to the spur a sword, a gold-laced mantle and a grant of money, in return for which there is no doubt that regular service was required.

The patronage of art and letters for which this court has obtained a world-wide reputation was exercised through the university, which was one of the most perfect in Italy, and by the gift of places in the personal or official service of the prince; it involved consequently no additional expense. Boiardo, as a wealthy country gentleman and high official, belonged to this class. At the time when Ariosto began to distinguish himself, there existed no court, in the true sense of the word, either at Milan or Florence, and soon there was none either at Urbino or at Naples. He had to content himself with a place among the musicians and jugglers of Cardinal Ippolito till Alfonso took him into his service. It was otherwise at a later time with Torquato Tasso, whose presence at court was jealously sought after.

The Opponents of the Despots

In face of this centralized authority, all legal opposition within the borders of the state was futile. The elements needed for the restoration of a republic had been for ever destroyed, and the field prepared for violence and despotism. The nobles, destitute of political rights, even where they held feudal possessions, might call themselves Guelphs or Ghibellines at will, might dress up their bravos in padded hose and feathered caps or how else they pleased; thoughtful men like Machiavelli knew well enough that Milan and Naples were too 'corrupt' for a republic. Strange judgements fall on these two so-called parties, which now served only to give an official sanction to personal and family disputes. An Italian prince, whom Agrippa of Nettesheim advised to put them down, replied that their quarrels brought him more than 12,000 ducats a year in fines. And when in the year 1500, during the brief return of Lodovico il Moro to his states, the Guelphs of Tortona summoned a part of the neighbouring French army into the city, in order to make an end once for all of their opponents, the French certainly began by plundering and ruining the Ghibellines, but finished by doing the same to the Guelphs, till Tortona was utterly laid waste. In Romagna, the hotbed of every ferocious passion, these two names had long lost all political meaning. It was a sign of the political delusion of the people that they not seldom believed the Guelphs to be the natural allies of the French and the Ghibellines of the Spaniards. It is hard to see that those who tried to profit by this error got much by doing so. France, after all her interventions, had to abandon the peninsula at last, and what became of Spain, after she had destroyed Italy, is known to every reader.

But to return to the despots of the Renaissance. A pure and simple mind, we might think, would perhaps have argued that, since all power is derived from God, these princes, if they were loyally and honestly supported by all their subjects, must in time themselves improve and lose all traces of their violent origin. But from characters and imaginations inflamed by passion and ambition, reasoning of this kind could not be expected. Like bad physicians, they thought to cure the disease by removing the symptoms, and fancied that if the tyrant were put to death, freedom would follow of itself. Or else, without reflecting even to this extent, they sought only to give a vent to the universal hatred, or to take vengeance for some family misfortune or personal affront. Since the governments were absolute, and free from all legal restraints, the opposition chose its weapons with equal freedom. Boccaccio declares openly:

> Shall I call the tyrant king or prince, and obey him loyally as my lord? No, for he is the enemy of the commonwealth. Against him I may use arms, conspiracies, spies, ambushes and fraud; to do so is a sacred and necessary work. There is no more acceptable sacrifice than the blood of a tyrant.

We need not occupy ourselves with individual cases; Machiavelli, in a famous chapter of his *Discorsi*, treats of the conspiracies of ancient and modern times from the days of the Greek tyrants downwards, and classifies them with cold-blooded indifference according to their various plans and results. We need make but two observations, first on the murders committed in church, and next on the influence of classical antiquity. So well was the tyrant guarded that it was almost impossible to lay hands upon him elsewhere than at solemn religious services; and on no other occasion was the whole family to be found assembled together. It was thus that the Fabrianese murdered the members of their ruling house, the Chiavelli, during high mass (1435), the signal being given by the words of the Creed, *'Et incarnatus est.'* At Milan the Duke Giovan Maria Visconti (1412) was assassinated at the entrance of the church of San Gottardo, Galeazzo Maria Sforza (1476) in the church of Santo Stefano, and Lodovico il Moro only escaped (1484) the daggers of the adherents of the widowed Duchess Bona through entering the church of Sant' Ambrogio by another door than that by which he was expected. There was no intentional impiety in the act; the assassins of Galeazzo did not fail to pray before the murder to the patron saint of the church, and to listen devoutly to the first mass. It was, however, one cause of the partial failure of the conspiracy of the Pazzi against Lorenzo and Giuliano Medici (1478), that the brigand Montesecco, who had bargained to commit the murder at a banquet, declined to undertake it in the cathedral of Florence. Certain of the clergy 'who were familiar with the sacred place, and consequently had no fear' were induced to act in his stead.

As to the imitation of antiquity, the influence of which

on moral and more especially on political questions we shall often refer to, the example was set by the rulers themselves, who, both in their conception of the state and in their personal conduct, took the old Roman empire avowedly as their model. In like manner their opponents, when they set to work with a deliberate theory, took pattern by the ancient tyrannicides. It may be hard to prove that in the main point – in forming the resolve itself – they consciously followed a classical example; but the appeal to antiquity was no mere phrase. The most striking disclosures have been left us with respect to the murderers of Galeazzo Sforza – Lampugnani, Olgiati and Visconti. Though all three had personal ends to serve, yet their enterprise may be partly ascribed to a more general reason. About this time Cola de' Montani, a humanist and professor of eloquence, had awakened among many of the young Milanese nobility a vague passion for glory and patriotic achievements, and had mentioned to Lampugnani and Olgiati his hope of delivering Milan. Suspicion was soon aroused against him: he was banished from the city, and his pupils were abandoned to the fanaticism he had excited. Some ten days before the deed they met together and took a solemn oath in the monastery of Sant' Ambrogio. 'Then,' says Olgiati, 'in a remote corner I raised my eyes before the picture of the patron saint, and implored his help for ourselves and for all *his* people.' The heavenly protector of the city was called on to bless the undertaking, as was afterwards St Stephen, in whose church it was fulfilled. Many of their comrades were now informed of the plot, nightly meetings were held in the house of Lampugnani, and the conspirators practised for the murder with the sheaths of their daggers. The attempt was successful, but Lampugnani was killed on the spot by the attendants of the duke; the others were captured. Visconti was penitent, but Olgiati through all his tortures maintained that the deed was an acceptable offering to God, and exclaimed while the executioner was breaking his ribs, 'Courage, Girolamo! Thou wilt long be remembered; death is bitter, but glory is eternal.'

But however idealistic the object and purpose of such conspiracies may appear, the manner in which they were conducted betrays the influence of that worst of all conspirators, Catiline – a man in whose thoughts freedom had no place whatever. The annals of Siena tell us expressly that the conspirators were students of Sallust, and the fact is indirectly confirmed by the confession of Olgiati. Elsewhere, too, we meet with the name of Catiline, and a more attractive pattern of the conspirator, apart from the end he followed, could hardly be discovered.

Among the Florentines, whenever they got rid of, or tried to get rid of, the Medici, tyrannicide was a practice universally accepted and approved. After the flight of the Medici in 1494, the bronze group of Donatello – Judith with the dead Holofernes – was taken from their collection, and placed before the Palazzo della Signoria, on the spot where the *David* of Michelangelo now stands, with the inscription, '*Exemplum salutis publicae cives posuere* 1495'. No example was more popular than that of the younger Brutus, who, in Dante, lies with Cassius and Judas Iscariot in the lowest pit of hell, because of his treason to the empire. Pietro Paolo Boscoli, whose plot against Giuliano, Giovanni and Giulio Medici failed (1513), was an enthusiastic admirer of Brutus, and in order to follow his steps, only waited to find a Cassius. Such a partner he met with in Agostino Capponi. His last utterances in prison – a striking evidence of the religious feeling of the time – show with what an effort he rid his mind of these classical imaginations, in order to die like a Christian. A friend and the confessor both had to assure him that St Thomas Aquinas condemned conspirators absolutely; but the confessor afterwards admitted to the same friend that St Thomas drew a distinction and permitted conspiracies against a tyrant who had forced himself on a people against their will.

After Lorenzino Medici had murdered the Duke Alessandro (1537), and then escaped, an apology for the deed appeared, which is probably his own work, and certainly composed in his interest, in which he praises tyrannicide as an act of the highest merit; on the supposition that Alessandro was a legitimate Medici, and, therefore, related to him, if only distantly, he boldly compares himself with Timoleon, who slew his brother for his country's sake. Others, on the same occasion, made use of the comparison with Brutus, and that Michelangelo himself, even late in life, was not unfriendly to ideas of this kind, may be inferred from his bust of Brutus in the Bargello. He left it unfinished, like nearly all his works, but certainly not because the murder of Cesare was repugnant to his feeling, as the couplet beneath declares.

A popular radicalism in the form in which it is opposed to the monarchies of later times is not to be found in the despotic states of the Renaissance. Each individual protested inwardly against despotism but was rather disposed to make tolerable or profitable terms with it, than to combine with others for its destruction. Things must have been as bad as at Camerino, Fabriano or Rimini before the citizens united to destroy or expel the ruling house. They knew in most cases only too well that this would but mean a change of masters. The star of the republics was certainly on the decline.

The Republics: Venice and Florence

The Italian municipalities had, in earlier days, given signal proof of that force which transforms the city into the state. It remained only that these cities should combine in a great confederation; and this idea was constantly recurring to Italian statesmen, whatever differences of form it might from time to time display. In fact, during the struggles of the twelfth and thirteenth centuries, great and formidable leagues actually were formed by the cities; and Sismondi is of the opinion that the time of the final armaments of the Lombard confederation against Barbarossa (from 1168 on) was the moment when a universal Italian league was possible. But the more powerful states had already developed characteristic features which made any such scheme impracticable. In their commercial dealings they shrank from no measures, however extreme, which might damage their competitors; they held their weaker neighbours in a condition of helpless dependence – in short, they each fancied they could get on by themselves without the assistance of the rest, and thus paved the way for future usurpation. The usurper was forthcoming when long conflicts between the nobility and the people, and between the different factions of the nobility, had awakened the desire for a strong government, and when bands of mercenaries ready and willing to sell their aid to the highest bidder had superseded the general levy of the citizens, which party leaders now found unsuited to their purposes. The tyrants destroyed the freedom of most of the cities; here and there they were expelled, but not thoroughly, or only for a short time; and they were always restored, since the inward conditions were favourable to them, and the opposing forces were exhausted.

Among the cities which maintained their independence are two of deep significance for the history of the human race: Florence, the city of incessant movement, which has left us a record of the thoughts and aspirations of each and all who, for three centuries, took part in this movement, and Venice, the city of apparent stagnation and of political secrecy. No contrast can be imagined stronger than that which is offered us by these two, and neither can be compared to anything else which the world had hitherto produced.

Venice recognized itself from the first as a strange and mysterious creation – the fruits of a higher power than human ingenuity. The solemn foundation of the city was the subject of a legend. On 25 March 413, at midday, the emigrants from Padua laid the first stone at the Rialto, that they might have a sacred, inviolable asylum amid the devastations of the barbarians. Later writers attributed to the founders the presentiment of the future greatness of the city; M. Antonio Sabellico, who has celebrated the event in the dignified flow of his hexameters, makes the priest who completes the act of consecration cry to heaven, 'When we hereafter attempt great things, grant us prosperity! Now we kneel before a poor altar; but if our vows are not made in vain, a hundred temples, O God, of gold and marble shall arise to Thee.' The island city at the end of the fifteenth century was the jewel-casket of the world. It is so described by the same Sabellico, with its ancient cupolas, its leaning towers, its inlaid marble façades, its compressed splendour, when the richest decoration did not hinder the practical employment of every corner of space. He takes us to the crowded piazza before San Giacometto at the Rialto, where the business of the world is transacted, not amid shouting and confusion, but with the subdued hum of many voices; where in the porticoes round the square and in those of the adjoining streets sit hundreds of money-changers and goldsmiths, with endless rows of shops and warehouses above their heads. He describes the great Fondaco of the Germans beyond the bridge, where their goods and their dwellings lay, and before which their ships are drawn up side by side in the canal; higher up is a whole fleet laden with wine and oil, and parallel with it, on the shore swarming with porters, are the vaults of the merchants; then from the Rialto to the square of St Mark come the inns and the perfumers' cabinets. So he conducts the reader from one quarter of the city to another till he comes at last to the two hospitals which were among those institutions of public utility nowhere so numerous as at Venice. Care for the people, in peace as well as in war, was characteristic of this government, and its attention to the wounded, even to those of the enemy, excited the admiration of other states.

Public institutions of every kind found in Venice their pattern; the pensioning of retired servants was carried out systematically, and included a provision for widows and orphans. Wealth, political security and acquaintance with other countries had matured the understanding of such questions. These slender fair-haired men with quiet cautious steps and deliberate speech differed but slightly in costume and bearing from one another; ornaments, especially pearls, were reserved for the women and girls. At that time the general prosperity, notwithstanding the losses sustained from the Turks, was still dazzling; the stores of energy which the city possessed and the prejudice in its favour diffused throughout Europe enabled it at a much later time to survive the heavy blows which were inflicted by the discovery of the sea route to the Indies, by the fall of the Mamelukes in Egypt, and by the war of the League of Cambrai.

Sabellico, born in the neighbourhood of Tivoli, and accustomed to the frank loquacity of the scholars of his day, remarks elsewhere with some astonishment that the young nobles who came of a morning to hear his lectures could not be prevailed on to enter into political discussions. 'When I ask them what people think, say and expect about this or that movement in Italy, they all answer with one voice that they know nothing about the matter.' Still, in spite of the strict imposition of the state, much was to be learned from the more corrupt members of the aristocracy by those who were willing to pay enough for it. In the last quarter of the fifteenth century there were traitors among the highest officials; the popes, the Italian princes, and even second-rate *condottieri* in the service of the government had informers in their pay, sometimes with regular salaries; things went so far that the Council of Ten found it prudent to conceal important political news from the Council of the Pregadi, and it was even supposed that Lodovico il Moro had control of a definite number of votes among the latter. Whether the hanging of single offenders and the high rewards – such as a life-pension of sixty ducats paid to those who informed against them – were of much avail, it is hard to decide; one of the chief causes of this evil, the poverty of many of the nobility, could not be removed in a day. In the year 1492 a proposal was urged by two of that order, that the state should spend 70,000 ducats for the relief of those poorer nobles who held no public office; the matter was near coming before the Great Council, in which it might have had a majority, when the Council of Ten interfered in time and banished the two proposers for life to Nicosia in Cyprus. About this time a Soranzo was hanged, though not in Venice itself, for sacrilege, and a Contarini put in chains for burglary; another of the same family came in 1499 before the Signoria, and complained that for many years he had been without an office, that he had only sixteen ducats a year and nine children, that his debts amounted to sixty ducats, that he knew no trade and had lately been turned on to the streets. We can understand why some of the wealthier nobles built houses, sometimes whole rows of them, to provide free lodging for their needy comrades. Such works figure in wills among deeds of charity.

But if the enemies of Venice ever founded serious hopes upon abuses of this kind, they were greatly in error. It might be thought that the commercial activity of the city, which put within reach of the humblest a rich reward for their labour, and the colonies on the eastern shores of the Mediterranean would have diverted from political affairs the dangerous elements of society. But had not the political history of Genoa, notwithstanding similar advantages, been of the stormiest? The cause of the stability of Venice lies rather in a combination of circumstances which were found in union nowhere else. Unassailable from its position, it had been able from the beginning to treat of foreign affairs with the fullest and calmest reflection and ignore nearly altogether the parties which divided the rest of Italy, to escape the entanglement of permanent alliances, and to set the highest price on those which it thought fit to make. The keynote of the Venetian character was, consequently, a spirit of proud and contemptuous isolation, which, joined to the hatred felt for the city by the other states of Italy, gave rise to a strong sense of solidarity within. The inhabitants meanwhile were united by the most powerful ties of interest in dealing both with the colonies and with the possessions on the mainland, forcing the population of the latter, that is, of all the towns up to Bergamo, to buy and sell in Venice alone. A power which rested on means so artificial could only be maintained by internal harmony and unity; and this conviction was so widely diffused among the citizens that the conspirator found few elements to work upon. And the discontented, if there were such, were held so far apart by the division between the noble and the burgher that a mutual understanding was not easy. On the other hand, within the ranks of the nobility itself, travel, commercial enterprise and the incessant wars with the Turks saved the wealthy and dangerous from that fruitful source of conspiracies – idleness. In these wars they were spared, often to a criminal extent, by the general in command, and the fall of the city was predicted by a Venetian Cato, if this fear of the nobles 'to give one another pain' should continue at the expense of justice. Nevertheless this free movement in the open air gave the Venetian aristocracy, as a whole, a healthy bias.

And when envy and ambition called for satisfaction an official victim was forthcoming, and legal means and authorities were ready. The moral torture, which for years the Doge Francesco Foscari (d. 1457) suffered before the eyes of all Venice, is a frightful example of a vengeance possible only in an aristocracy. The Council of Ten, which had a hand in everything, which disposed without appeal of life and death, of financial affairs and military appointments, which included the Inquisitors among its number, and which overthrew Foscari, as it had overthrown so many powerful men before – this council was yearly chosen afresh from the whole governing body, the Gran Consiglio, and was consequently the most direct expression of its will. It is not probable that serious intrigues occurred at these elections, as the short duration of the office and the accountability which followed rendered it an object of no great desire. But violent and mysterious as the proceedings of this and other authorities might be, the genuine Venetian courted rather than fled their sentence, not only because the republic had long arms, and if it could not catch him might punish his family, but because in most cases it acted from rational motives and not from a thirst for blood. No state, indeed, has ever exercised a greater moral influence over its subjects, whether abroad or at home. If traitors were to be found among the Pregadi, there was ample compensation for this in the fact that every Venetian away from home was a born spy for his government. It was a matter of course that the Venetian cardinals at Rome sent home news of the transactions of the secret papal consistories. The Cardinal Domenico Grimani had the dispatches intercepted in the neighbourhood of Rome (1500) which Ascanio Sforza was sending to his brother Lodovico il Moro, and forwarded them to Venice; his father, then exposed to a serious accusation, claimed public credit for this service of his son before the Gran Consiglio; in other words, before all the world.

The conduct of the Venetian government to the *condottieri* in its pay has been spoken of already. The only further guarantee of their fidelity which could be obtained lay in their great number, by which treachery was made as difficult as its discovery was easy. In looking at the Venetian army list, one is only surprised that among forces of such miscellaneous composition any common action was possible. In the catalogue for the campaign of 1495 we find 15,526 horsemen, broken up into a number of small divisions. Gonzaga of Mantua alone had as many as 1,200, and Gioffredo Borgia 740; then follow six officers with a contingent of 600 to 700, ten with 400, twelve with 400 to 200, fourteen or thereabouts with 200 to 100, nine with 80, six with 50 to 60, and so forth. These forces were partly composed of old Venetian troops, partly of veterans led by Venetian city or country nobles; the majority of the leaders were, however, princes and rulers of cities or their relatives. To these forces must be added 24,000 infantry – we are not told how they were raised or commanded – with 3,300 additional troops, who probably belonged to the special services. In time of peace the cities of the mainland were wholly unprotected or occupied by insignificant garrisons. Venice relied, if not exactly on the loyalty, at least on the good sense of its subjects; in the war of the League of Cambrai (1509) it absolved them, as is well known, from their oath of allegiance, and let them compare the amenities of a foreign occupation with the mild government to which they had been accustomed. As there had been no treason in their desertion of St Mark, and consequently no punishment was to be feared, they returned to their old masters with the utmost eagerness. This war, we may remark parenthetically, was the result of a century's outcry against the Venetian desire for aggrandizement. The Venetians, in fact, were not free from the mistake of those over-clever people who will credit their opponents with no irrational and inconsiderate conduct. Misled by this optimism, which is, perhaps, a peculiar weakness of aristocracies, they had utterly ignored not only the preparations of Muhammad II for the capture of Constantinople, but even the armaments of Charles VIII, till the unexpected blow fell at last. The League of Cambrai was an event of the same character, in so far as it was clearly opposed to the interests of the two chief members, Louis XII and Julius II. The hatred of all Italy against the victorious city seemed to be concentrated in the mind of the pope, and to have blinded him to the evils of foreign intervention; and as to the policy of Cardinal d'Amboise and his king, Venice ought long before to have recognized it as a piece of malicious imbecility, and to have been thoroughly on its guard. The other members of the League took part in it from that envy which may be a salutary corrective to great wealth and power, but which in itself is a beggarly sentiment. Venice came out of the conflict with honour, but not without lasting damage.

A power, whose foundations were so complicated, whose activity and interests filled so wide a stage, cannot be imagined without a systematic oversight of the whole, without a regular estimate of means and burdens, of profits and losses. Venice can fairly make good its claim to be the birthplace of statistical science, together, perhaps, with Florence, and followed by the more enlightened despotisms. The feudal state of the Middle Ages knew of nothing more than catalogues of signorial rights and possessions (*urbaria*); it looked on production as a fixed quantity, which it approximately is, so long as we have to do with landed property only. The towns, on the other hand, throughout the West must from very early times have treated production, which with them depended on industry and commerce, as exceedingly variable; but, even in the most flourishing times of the Hanseatic League, they never got beyond a simple commercial balance-sheet. Fleets, armies, political power and influence fall under the debit and credit of a trader's ledger. In the Italian states a clear political consciousness, the pattern of Muhammadan administration, and the long and active exercise of trade and commerce combined to produce for the first time a true science of statistics. The absolute monarchy of Frederick II in Lower Italy was organized with the sole object of securing a concentrated power for the death-struggle in which he was engaged. In Venice, on the contrary, the supreme objects were the enjoyment of life and power, the increase of inherited advantages, the creation of the most lucrative forms of industry, and the opening of new channels for commerce.

The writers of the time speak of these things with the greatest freedom. We learn that the population of the city amounted in the year 1422 to 190,000 souls; the Italians were, perhaps, the first to reckon, not according to hearths, or men able to bear arms, or people able to walk, and so forth, but according to *animae*, and thus to get the most neutral basis for further calculation. About this time, when the Florentines wished to form an alliance with Venice against Filippo Maria Visconti, they were for the moment refused, in the belief, resting on accurate commercial returns, that a war between Venice and Milan, that is, between seller and buyer, was foolish. Even if the duke simply increased his army, the Milanese, through the heavier taxation they must pay, would become worse customers. 'Better let the Florentines be defeated, and then, used as they are to the life of a free city, they will settle with us and bring their silk and woollen industry with them, as the Lucchese did in their distress.' The speech of the dying Doge Mocenigo (1423) to a few of the senators whom he had sent for to his bedside is still more remarkable. It contains the chief elements of a statistical account of the whole resources of Venice. I cannot say whether or where a thorough elucidation of this perplexing document exists; by way of illustration, the following facts may be quoted. After repaying a war-loan of four million ducats, the public debt (*il monte*) still amounted to six million ducats; the current trade (so it seems) ten million, which yielded, the text informs us, a profit of four million. The 3,000 *navigli*, the 300 *navi*, and the 45 galleys were manned respectively by 17,000, 8,000 and 11,000 seamen (more than 200 for each galley). To these must be added 16,000 shipwrights. The houses in Venice were valued at seven million, and brought in a rent of half a million. There were 1,000 nobles whose income ranged from 70 to 4,000 ducats. In another passage the ordinary income of the state in that same year is put at 1,100,000 ducats; through the disturbance of trade caused by the wars it sank about the middle of the century to 800,000 ducats.

If Venice, by this spirit of calculation, and by the practical turn which she gave it, was the first fully to represent one important side of modern political life, in that culture, on the other hand, which Italy then prized most highly she did not stand in the front rank. The literary impulse, in general, was here wanting, and especially that enthusiasm for classical antiquity which prevailed elsewhere. The aptitude of the Venetians, says Sabellico, for philosophy and eloquence was in itself not less remarkable than for commerce and politics. George of Trebizond, who, in 1459, laid the Latin translation of Plato's *Laws* at the feet of the doge, was appointed professor of philology with a yearly salary of 150 ducats, and finally dedicated his *Rhetoric* to the Signoria. If, however, we look through the history of Venetian literature which Francesco Sansovino has appended to his well-known book, we shall find in the fourteenth century almost nothing but history, and special works on theology, jurisprudence and medicine; and in the fifteenth century, till we come to Ermolao Barbaro and Aldo Manucci, humanistic culture is, for a city of such importance, most scantily represented. The library which Cardinal Bessarion bequeathed to the state (1468) narrowly escaped dispersion and destruction. Learning was certainly cultivated at the university of Padua, where, however, the physicians and the jurists – the latter as the authors of legal opinions – received by far the highest pay. The share of Venice in the poetical creations of the country was long insignificant, till, at the beginning of the sixteenth century, her deficiencies were made good. Even the art of the Renaissance was imported into the city from without, and it was not before the end of the fifteenth century that she learned to move in this field with independent freedom and strength. But we find more striking instances still of intellectual backwardness. This government, which had the clergy so thoroughly in its control, which reserved to itself the appointment to all important ecclesiastical offices, and which, one time after another, dared to defy the court of Rome, displayed an official piety of a most singular kind. The bodies of saints and other relics imported from Greece after the Turkish conquest were bought at the greatest sacrifices and received by the doge in solemn procession. For the coat without a seam it was decided (1455) to offer 10,000 ducats, but it was not to be had. These measures were not the fruit of any popular excitement, but of the tranquil resolutions of the heads of the government, and might have been omitted without attracting any comment, and at Florence, under similar circumstances, would certainly have been omitted. We shall say nothing of the piety of the masses, and of their firm belief in the indulgences of an Alexander VI. But the state itself, after absorbing the Church to a degree unknown elsewhere, had in truth a certain ecclesiastical element in its composition, and the doge, the symbol of the state, appeared in twelve great processions (*andate*) in a half-clerical character. They were almost all festivals in memory of political events, and competed in splendour with the great feasts of the Church; the most brilliant of all, the famous marriage with the sea, fell on Ascension Day.

The most elevated political thought and the most varied forms of human development are found united in the history of Florence, which in this sense deserves the name of the most modern state in the world. Here the whole people are busied with what in the despotic cities is the affair of a single family. That wondrous Florentine spirit, at once keenly critical and artistically creative, was incessantly transforming the social and political condition of the state, and as incessantly describing and judging the change. Florence thus became the home of political doctrines and theories, of experiments and sudden changes, but also, like Venice, the home of statistical science, and alone and above all other states in the world, the home of historical representation in the modern sense of the phrase. The spectacle of ancient Rome and a familiarity with its leading writers were not without influence; Giovanni Villani confesses that he received the first impulse to his great work at the jubilee of the year 1300, and began it immediately on his return home. Yet how many among the 200,000 pilgrims of that year may have been like him in gifts and tendencies and still did not write the history of their native cities! For not all of them could encourage themselves with the thought, 'Rome is sinking; my native city is rising, and ready to achieve great things, and therefore I wish to relate its past history, and hope to continue the story to the present time, and as long as my life shall last.' And besides the witness to its past, Florence obtained through its historians something further – a greater fame than fell to the lot of any other city of Italy.

Our present task is not to write the history of this remarkable state, but merely to give a few indications of the intellectual freedom and independence for which the Florentines were indebted to this history.

In no other city of Italy were the struggles of political parties so bitter, of such early origin, and so permanent. The descriptions of them, which belong, it is true, to a somewhat later period, give clear evidence of the superiority of Florentine criticism.

And what a politician is the great victim of these crises, Dante Alighieri, matured alike by home and by exile! He uttered his scorn of the incessant changes and experiments in the constitution of his native city in verses of adamant, which will remain proverbial so long as political events of the same kind recur; he addressed his home in words of defiance and yearning which must have stirred the hearts of his countrymen. But his thoughts ranged over Italy and the whole world; and if his passion for the Empire, as he conceived it, was no more than an illusion, it must yet be admitted that the youthful dreams of a newborn political speculation are in his case not without a poetical grandeur. He is proud to be the first who trod this path, certainly in the footsteps of Aristotle, but in his own way independently. His ideal emperor is a just and humane judge, dependent on God only, the heir of the universal sway of Rome to which belonged the sanction of nature, of right and of the will of God. The conquest of the world was, according to this view, rightful, resting on a divine judgement between Rome and the other nations of the earth, and God gave his approval to this Empire, since under it he became Man, submitting at his birth to the census of the Emperor Augustus, and at his death to the judgement of Pontius Pilate. We may find it hard to appreciate these and other arguments of the same kind, but Dante's passion never fails to carry us with him. In his letters he appears as one of the earliest publicists, and is perhaps the first layman to publish political tracts in this form. He began early. Soon after the death of Beatrice he addressed a pamphlet on the state of Florence 'to the Great ones of the Earth', and the public utterances of his later years, dating from the time of his banishment, are all directed to emperors, princes and cardinals. In these letters and in his book *De Vulgari Eloquio* the feeling, bought with such bitter pains, is constantly recurring that the exile may find elsewhere than in his native place an intellectual home in language and culture, which cannot be taken from him. On this point we shall have more to say in the sequel.

To the two Villani, Giovanni as well as Matteo, we owe not so much deep political reflection as fresh and practical observations, together with the elements of Florentine statistics and important notices of other states. Here too trade and commerce had given the impulse to economical as well as political science. Nowhere else in the world was such accurate information to be had on financial affairs. The wealth of the papal court at Avignon, which at the death of John XXII amounted to 25 million gold florins, would be incredible on any less trustworthy authority. Here only, at Florence, do we meet with colossal loans like that which the King of England contracted from the Florentine houses of Bardi and Peruzzi, who lost to His Majesty the sum of 1,365,000 gold florins (1338) – their own money and that of their partners – and nevertheless recovered from the shock. Most important facts are here recorded as to the condition of Florence at this time: the public income (over 300,000 gold florins) and expenditure; the population of the city, here only roughly estimated, according to the consumption of bread, in *bocche*, i.e. mouths, put at 90,000, and the population of the whole territory; the excess of 300 to 500 male children among the 5,800 to 6,000 annually baptized; the schoolchildren, of whom 8,000 to 10,000 learned reading, 1,000 to 1,200 in six schools arithmetic; and besides these, 600 scholars who were taught Latin grammar and logic in four schools. Then follow the statistics of the churches and monasteries; of the hospitals, which held more than a thousand beds; of the wool-trade, with its most valuable details; of the mint, the provisioning of the city, the public officials, and so on. Incidentally we learn many curious facts; how, for instance, when the public funds (*monte*) were first established, in the year 1353, the Franciscans spoke from the pulpit in favour of the measure, the Dominicans and Augustinians against it. The economical results of the black death were and could be observed and described nowhere else in all Europe as in this city. Only a Florentine could have left it on record how it was expected that the scanty population would have made everything cheap, and how instead of that labour and commodities doubled in price; how the common people at first would do no work at all, but simply gave themselves up to enjoyment; how in the city itself servants and maids were not to be had except at extravagant wages; how the peasants would only till the best lands, and left the rest uncultivated; and how the enormous legacies bequeathed to the poor at the time of the plague seemed afterwards useless, since the poor had either died or had ceased to be poor. Lastly, on the occasion of a great bequest, by which a childless philanthropist left six *danari* to every beggar in the city, the attempt is made to give a comprehensive statistical account of Florentine mendicancy.

This statistical view of things was at a later time still more highly cultivated at Florence. The noteworthy point about it is that, as a rule, we can perceive its connection with the higher aspects of history, with art, and with culture in general. An inventory of the year 1422 mentions, within the compass of the same document, the seventy-two exchange offices which surrounded the Mercato Nuovo; the amount of coined money in circulation (2 million golden florins); the then new industry of gold spinning; the silk wares; Filippo Brunellesco, then busy in digging classical architecture from its grave; and Leonardo Aretino, secretary of the republic, at work at the revival of ancient literature and eloquence; lastly, it speaks of the general prosperity of the city, then free from political conflicts, and of the good fortune of Italy, which had rid itself of foreign mercenaries. The Venetian statistics quoted above, which date from about the same year, certainly give evidence of larger property and profits and of a more extensive scene of action; Venice had long been mistress of the seas before Florence sent out its first galleys (1422) to Alexandria. But no reader can fail to recognize the higher spirit of the Florentine documents. These and similar lists recur at intervals of ten years, systematically arranged and tabulated, while elsewhere we find at best occasional notices. We can form an approximate estimate of the property and the business of the first Medici; they paid for charities, public buildings and taxes from 1434 to 1471 no less than 663,755 gold florins, of which more than 400,000 fell on Cosimo alone, and Lorenzo il Magnifico was delighted that the money had been so well spent. In 1478 we have again a most important and in its way complete view of the commerce and trades of this city, some of which may be wholly or partly reckoned among the fine arts – such as those which had to do with damasks and gold or silver embroidery, with woodcarving and intarsia, with the sculpture of arabesques in marble and sandstone, with portraits in wax, and with jewellery and work in gold. The inborn talent of the Florentines for the systematization of outward life is shown by their books on agriculture, business and domestic economy, which are markedly superior to those of other European people in the fifteenth century. It has been rightly decided to publish selections of these works, although no little study will be needed to extract clear and definite results from them. At all events, we have no difficulty in recognizing the city, where dying parents begged the government in their wills to fine their sons 1,000 florins if they declined to practise a regular profession.

For the first half of the sixteenth century probably no state in the world possesses a document like the magnificent description of Florence by Varchi. In descriptive statistics, as in so many things besides, yet another model is left to us, before the freedom and greatness of the city sank into the grave.

This statistical estimate of outward life is, however, uniformly accompanied by the narrative of political events to which we have already referred.

Florence not only existed under political forms more varied than those of the free states of Italy and of Europe generally, but it reflected upon them far more deeply. It is a faithful mirror of the relations of individuals and classes to a variable whole. The pictures of the great civic democracies in France and in Flanders, as they are delineated in Froissart, and the narratives of the German chroniclers of the fourteenth century, are in truth of high importance; but in comprehensiveness of thought and in the rational development of the story none will bear comparison with the Florentines. The rule of the nobility, the tyrannies, the struggles of the middle class with the proletariat, limited and unlimited democracy, pseudo-democracy, the primacy of a single house, the theocracy of Savonarola, and the mixed forms of government which prepared the way for the Medicean despotism – all are so described that the inmost motives of the actors are laid bare to the light. At length Machiavelli in his Florentine history (down to 1492) represents his native city as a living organism and its development as a natural and individual process; he is the first of the moderns who has risen to such a conception. It lies without our province to determine whether and in what points Machiavelli may have done violence to history, as is notoriously the case in his life of Castruccio Castracani – a fancy picture of the typical despot. We might find something to say against every line of the *Storie Fiorentine*, and yet the great and unique value of the whole would remain unaffected. And his contemporaries and successors, Jacopo Pitti, Guicciardini, Segni, Varchi, Vettori, what a circle of illustrious names! And what a story it is which these masters tell us! The great and memorable drama of the last decades of the Florentine republic is here unfolded. The voluminous record of the collapse of the highest and most original life which the world could then show may appear to one but as a collection of curiosities, may awaken in another a devilish delight at the shipwreck of so much nobility and grandeur, to a third may seem like a great historical assize; for all it will be an object of thought and study to the end of time. The evil, which was for ever troubling the peace of the city, was its rule over once powerful and now conquered rivals like Pisa – a rule of which the necessary consequence was a chronic state of violence. The only remedy, certainly an extreme one and which none but Savonarola could have persuaded Florence to accept, and that only with the help of favourable chances, would have been the well-timed dissolution of Tuscany into a federal union of free cities. At a later period this scheme, then no more than the dream of a past age, brought (1548) a patriotic citizen of Lucca to the scaffold. From this evil and from the ill-starred Guelph sympathies of Florence for a foreign prince, which familiarized it with foreign intervention, came all the disasters which followed. But who does not admire the people, which was wrought up by its venerated preacher to a mood of such sustained loftiness, that for the first time in Italy it set the example of sparing a conquered foe, while the whole history of its past taught nothing but vengeance and extermination? The glow which melted patriotism into one with moral regeneration may seem, when looked at from a distance, to have soon passed away; but its best results shine forth again in the memorable siege of 1529–30. They were 'fools', as Guicciardini then wrote, who drew down this storm upon Florence, but he confesses himself that they achieved things which seemed incredible; and when he declares that sensible people would have got out of the way of the danger, he means no more than that Florence ought to have yielded itself silently and ingloriously into the hands of its enemies. It would no doubt have preserved its splendid suburbs and gardens, and the lives and prosperity of countless citizens; but it would have been the poorer by one of its greatest and most ennobling memories.

In many of their chief merits the Florentines are the pattern and the earliest type of Italians and modern Europeans generally; they are so also in many of their defects. When Dante compares the city which was always mending its constitution with the sick man who is continually changing his posture to escape from pain, he touches with the comparison a permanent feature of the political life of Florence. The great modern fallacy that a constitution can be made, can be manufactured by a combination of existing forces and tendencies, was constantly cropping up in stormy times; even Machiavelli is not wholly free from it. Constitutional artists were never wanting who by an ingenious distribution and division of political power, by indirect elections of the most complicated kind, by the establishment of nominal offices, sought to found a lasting order of things, and to satisfy or to deceive the rich and the poor alike. They naïvely fetch their examples from classical antiquity, and borrow the party names *ottimati*, *aristocrazia*, as a matter of course. The world since then has become used to these expressions and given them a conventional European sense, whereas all former party names were purely national, and either characterized the cause at issue or sprang from the caprice of accident. But how a name colours or discolours a political cause!

But of all who thought it possible to construct a state, the greatest beyond all comparison was Machiavelli. He treats existing forces as living and active, takes a large and an accurate view of alternative possibilities, and seeks to mislead neither himself nor others. No man could be freer from vanity or ostentation; indeed, he does not write for the public, but either for princes and administrators or for personal friends. The danger for him does not lie in an affectation of genius or in a false order of ideas, but rather in a powerful imagination which he evidently controls with difficulty. The objectivity of his political judgement is sometimes appalling in its sincerity; but it is the sign of a time of no ordinary need and peril, when it was a hard matter to believe in right, or to credit others with just dealing. Virtuous indignation at his expense is thrown away upon us who have seen in what sense political morality is understood by the statesmen of our own century. Machiavelli was at all events able to forget himself in his cause. In truth, although his writings, with the exception of very few words, are altogether destitute of enthusiasm, and although the Florentines themselves treated him at last as a criminal, he was a patriot in the fullest meaning of the word. But free as he was, like most of his contemporaries, in speech and morals, the welfare of the state was yet his first and last thought.

His most complete programme for the construction of a new political system at Florence is set forth in the memorial to Leo X, composed after the death of the younger Lorenzo Medici, Duke of Urbino (d. 1519), to whom he had dedicated his *Prince*. The state was by that time in extremities and utterly corrupt, and the remedies proposed are not always morally justifiable; but it is most interesting to see how he hopes to set up the republic in the form of a moderate democracy, as heiress to the Medici. A more ingenious scheme of concessions to the pope, to the pope's various adherents, and to the different Florentine interests cannot be imagined; we might fancy ourselves looking into the works of a clock. Principles, observations, comparisons, political forecasts and the like are to be found in numbers in the *Discorsi*, among them flashes of wonderful insight. He recognizes, for example, the law of a continuous though not uniform development in republican institutions, and requires the constitution to be flexible and capable of change, as the only means of dispensing with bloodshed and banishments. For a like reason, in order to guard against private violence and foreign interference – 'the death of all freedom' – he wishes to see introduced a judicial procedure (*accusa*) against hated citizens, in place of which Florence had hitherto had nothing but the court of scandal. With a masterly hand the tardy and involuntary decisions are characterized, which at critical moments play so important a part in republican states. Once, it is true, he is misled by his imagination and the pressure of events into unqualified praise of the people, which chooses its officers, he says, better than any prince, and which can be cured of its errors by 'good advice'. With regard to the government of Tuscany, he has no doubt that it belongs to his native city, and maintains, in a special *Discorso*, that the reconquest of Pisa is a question of life or death; he deplores that Arezzo, after the rebellion of 1502, was not razed to the ground; he admits in general that Italian republics must be allowed to expand freely and add to their territory in order to enjoy peace at home, and not to be themselves attacked by others, but declares that Florence had always begun at the wrong end, and from the first made deadly enemies of Pisa, Lucca and Siena, while Pistoia, 'treated like a brother', had voluntarily submitted to her.

It would be unreasonable to draw a parallel between the few other republics which still existed in the fifteenth century and this unique city – the most important workshop of the Italian, and indeed of the modern European spirit. Siena suffered from the gravest organic maladies, and its relative prosperity in art and industry must not mislead us on this point. Aeneas Sylvius looks with longing from his native town over to the 'merry' German imperial cities, where life is embittered by no confiscations of land and goods, by no arbitrary officials, and by no political factions. Genoa scarcely comes within range of our task, as before the time of Andrea Doria it took almost no part in the Renaissance. Indeed, the inhabitant of the Riviera was proverbial among Italians for his contempt of all higher culture. Party conflicts here assumed so fierce a character, and disturbed so violently the whole course of life, that we can hardly understand how, after so many revolutions and invasions, the Genoese ever contrived to return to an endurable condition. Perhaps it was owing to the fact that nearly all who took part in public affairs were at the same time almost without exception active men of business. The example of Genoa shows in a striking manner with what insecurity wealth and vast commerce, and with what internal disorder the possession of distant colonies, are compatible.

Lucca is of small significance in the fifteenth century.

Foreign Policy

As the majority of the Italian states were in their internal constitution works of art, that is, the fruit of reflection and careful adaptation, so was their relation to one another and to foreign countries also a work of art. That nearly all of them were the result of recent usurpations was a fact which exercised as fatal an influence in their foreign as in their internal policy. Not one of them recognized another without reserve; the same play of chance which had helped to found and consolidate one dynasty might upset another. Nor was it always a matter of choice with the despot whether to keep quiet or not. The necessity of movement and aggrandizement is common to all illegitimate powers. Thus Italy became the scene of a 'foreign policy' which gradually, as in other countries also, acquired the position of a recognized system of public law. The purely objective treatment of international affairs, as free from prejudice as from moral scruples, attained a perfection which sometimes is not without a certain beauty and grandeur of its own. But as a whole it gives us the impression of a bottomless abyss.

Intrigues, armaments, leagues, corruption and treason make up the outward history of Italy at this period. Venice in particular was long accused on all hands of seeking to conquer the whole peninsula, or gradually so to reduce its strength that one state after another must fall into her hands. But on a closer view it is evident that this complaint did not come from the people, but rather from the courts and official classes, which were commonly abhorred by their subjects, while the mild government of Venice had secured for it general confidence. Even Florence, with its restive subject cities, found itself in a false position with regard to Venice, apart from all commercial jealousy and from the progress of Venice in Romagna. At last the League of Cambrai actually did strike a serious blow at the state which all Italy ought to have supported with united strength.

The other states, also, were animated by feelings no less unfriendly, and were at all times ready to use against one another any weapon which their evil conscience might suggest. Lodovico il Moro, the Aragonese kings of Naples and Sixtus IV – to say nothing of the smaller powers – kept Italy in a constant perilous agitation. It would have been well if the atrocious game had been confined to Italy; but it lay in the nature of the case that intervention and help should at last be sought from abroad – in particular from the French and the Turks.

The sympathies of the people at large were throughout on the side of France. Florence had never ceased to confess with shocking *naïveté* its old Guelph preference for the French. And when Charles VIII actually appeared on the south of the Alps, all Italy accepted him with an enthusiasm which to himself and his followers seemed unaccountable. In the imagination of the Italians, to take Savonarola for an example, the ideal picture of a wise, just and powerful saviour and ruler was still living, with the difference that he was no longer the emperor invoked by Dante, but the Capetian King of France. With his departure the illusion was broken; but it was long before all understood how completely Charles VIII, Louis XII and Francis I had mistaken their true relation to Italy, and by what inferior motives they were led. The princes, for their part, tried to make use of France in a wholly different way. When the Franco-English wars came to an end, when Louis XI began to cast about his diplomatic nets on all sides, and Charles of Burgundy to embark on his foolish adventures, the Italian Cabinets came to meet them at every point. It became clear that the intervention of France was only a question of time, even though the claims on Naples and Milan had never existed, and that the old interference with Genoa and Piedmont was only a type of what was to follow. The Venetians, in fact, expected it as early as 1462. The mortal terror of the Duke Galeazzo Maria of Milan during the Burgundian war, in which he was apparently the ally of Charles as well as of Louis, and consequently had reason to dread an attack from both, is strikingly shown in his correspondence. The plan of an equilibrium of the four chief Italian powers, as understood by Lorenzo the Magnificent, was but the assumption of a cheerful optimistic spirit, which had outgrown both the recklessness of an experimental policy and the superstitions of Florentine Guelphism, and persisted in hoping for the best. When Louis XI offered him aid in the war against Ferrante of Naples and Sixtus IV, he replied, 'I cannot set my own advantage above the safety of all Italy; would to God it never came into the mind of the French kings to try their strength in this country! Should they ever do so, Italy is lost.' For the other princes, the King of France was alternately a bugbear to themselves and to their enemies, and they threatened to call him in whenever they saw no more convenient way out of their difficulties. The popes, in their turn, fancied that they could make use of France without any danger to themselves, and even Innocent VIII imagined that he could withdraw to sulk in the North, and return as a conqueror to Italy at the head of a French army.

Thoughtful men, indeed, foresaw the foreign conquest long before the expedition of Charles VIII. And when Charles was back again on the other side of the Alps, it was plain to every eye that an era of intervention had begun. Misfortune now followed on misfortune; it was understood too late that France and Spain, the two chief invaders, had become great European powers, that they would be no longer satisfied with verbal homage, but would fight to the death for influence and territory in Italy. They had begun to resemble the centralized Italian states, and indeed to copy them, only on a gigantic scale. Schemes of annexation or exchange of territory were for a time indefinitely multiplied. The end, as is well known, was the complete victory of Spain, which, as sword and shield of the Counter-Reformation, long held the papacy among its other subjects. The melancholy reflections of the philosophers could only show them how those who had called in the barbarians all came to a bad end.

Alliances were at the same time formed with the Turks too, with as little scruple or disguise; they were reckoned no worse than any other political expedients. The belief in the unity of Western Christendom had at various times in the course of the Crusades been seriously shaken, and

Frederick II had probably outgrown it. But the fresh advance of the oriental nations, the need and the ruin of the Greek empire, had revived the old feeling, though not in its former strength, throughout Western Europe. Italy, however, was a striking exception to this rule. Great as was the terror felt for the Turks, and the actual danger from them, there was yet scarcely a government of any consequence which did not conspire against other Italian states with Muhammad II and his successors. And when they did not do so, they still had the credit of it; nor was it worse than the sending of emissaries to poison the cisterns of Venice, which was the charge brought against the heirs of Alfonso, King of Naples. From a scoundrel like Sigismondo Malatesta nothing better could be expected than that he should call the Turks into Italy. But the Aragonese monarchs of Naples, from whom Muhammad – at the instigation, we read, of other Italian governments, especially of Venice – had once wrested Otranto (1480), afterwards hounded on the Sultan Bajazet II against the Venetians. The same charge was brought against Lodovico il Moro. 'The blood of the slain, and the misery of the prisoners in the hands of the Turks, cry to God for vengeance against him,' says the state historian. In Venice, where the government was informed of everything, it was known that Giovanni Sforza, ruler of Pesaro, the cousin of the Moor, had entertained the Turkish ambassadors on their way to Milan. The two most respectable among the popes of the fifteenth century, Nicholas V and Pius II, died in the deepest grief at the progress of the Turks, the latter indeed amid the preparations for a crusade which he was hoping to lead in person; their successors embezzled the contributions sent for this purpose from all parts of Christendom, and degraded the indulgences granted in return for them into a private commercial speculation. Innocent VIII consented to be gaoler to the fugitive Prince Djem, for a salary paid by the prisoner's brother Bajazet II, and Alexander VI supported the steps taken by Lodovico il Moro in Constantinople to further a Turkish assault upon Venice (1498), whereupon the latter threatened him with a Council. It is clear the notorious alliance between Francis I and Soliman II was nothing new or unheard of.

Indeed, we find instances of whole populations to whom it seemed no particular crime to go over bodily to the Turks. Even if it were only held out as a threat to oppressive governments, this is at least a proof that the idea had become familiar. As early as 1480 Battista Mantovano gives us clearly to understand that most of the inhabitants of the Adriatic coast foresaw something of this kind, and that Ancona in particular desired it. When Romagna was suffering from the oppressive government of Leo X, a deputy from Ravenna said openly to the legate, Cardinal Giulio Medici: 'Monsignore, the honourable Republic of Venice will not have us, for fear of a dispute with the Holy See; but if the Turk comes to Ragusa we will put ourselves into his hands.'

It was a poor but not wholly groundless consolation for the enslavement of Italy then begun by the Spaniards that the country was at least secured from the relapse into barbarism which would have awaited it under the Turkish rule. By itself, divided as it was, it could hardly have escaped this fate.

If, with all these drawbacks, the Italian statesmanship of this period deserves our praise, it is only on the ground of its practical and unprejudiced treatment of those questions which were not affected by fear, passion or malice, Here was no feudal system after the northern fashion, with its artificial scheme of rights; but the power which each possessed he held in practice as in theory. Here was no attendant nobility to foster in the mind of the prince the medieval sense of honour, with all its strange consequences; but princes and counsellors were agreed in acting according to the exigencies of the particular case and to the end they had in view. Towards the men whose services were used and towards allies, come from what quarter they might, no pride of caste was felt which could possibly estrange a supporter; and the class of the *condottieri*, in which birth was a matter of indifference, shows clearly enough in what sort of hands the real power lay; and lastly, the government, in the hands of an enlightened despot, had an incomparably more accurate acquaintance with its own country and that of its neighbours than was possessed by northern contemporaries, and estimated the economical and moral capacities of friend and foe down to the smallest particular. The rulers were, notwithstanding grave errors, born masters of statistical science. With such men negotiation was possible; it might be presumed that they would be convinced and their opinion modified when practical reasons were laid before them. When the great Alfonso of Naples was (1434) a prisoner of Filippo Maria Visconti, he was able to satisfy his gaoler that the rule of the House of Anjou instead of his own at Naples would make the French masters of Italy; Filippo Maria set him free without ransom and made an alliance with him. A northern prince would scarcely have acted in the same way, certainly not one whose morality in other respects was like that of Visconti. What confidence was felt in the power of self-interest is shown by the celebrated visit which Lorenzo the Magnificent, to the universal astonishment of the Florentines, paid the faithless Ferrante at Naples – a man who would be certainly tempted to keep him a prisoner, and was by no means too scrupulous to do so. For to arrest a powerful monarch, and then to let him go alive, after extorting his signature and otherwise insulting him, as Charles the Bold did to Louis XI at Peronne (1468), seemed madness to the Italians; so that Lorenzo was expected to come back covered with glory, or else not to come back at all. The art of political persuasion was at this time raised to a point – especially by the Venetian ambassadors – of which northern nations first obtained a conception from the Italians, and of which the official addresses give a most imperfect idea. These are mere pieces of humanistic rhetoric. Nor, in spite of an otherwise ceremonious etiquette, was there in case of need any lack of rough and frank speaking in diplomatic intercourse. A man like Machiavelli appears in his *Legazioni* in an almost pathetic light. Furnished with scanty instructions, shabbily equipped, and treated as an agent of inferior rank, he never loses his gift of free and wide observation or his pleasure in picturesque description.

A special division of this work will treat of the study of man individually and nationally, which among the Italians went hand in hand with the study of the outward conditions of human life.

War as a Work of Art

It must here be briefly indicated by what steps the art of war assumed the character of a product of reflection. Throughout the countries of the West the education of the individual soldier in the Middle Ages was perfect within the limits of the then prevalent system of defence and attack: nor was there any want of ingenious inventors in the arts of besieging and of fortification. But the development both of strategy and of tactics was hindered by the character and duration of military service, and by the ambition of the nobles, who disputed questions of precedence in the face of the enemy, and through simple want of discipline caused the loss of great battles like Crécy and Maupertuis. Italy, on the contrary, was the first country to adopt the system of mercenary troops, which demanded a wholly different organization; and the early introduction of firearms did its part in making war a democratic pursuit, not only because the strongest castles were unable to withstand a bombardment, but because the skill of the engineer, of the gun-founder and of the artillerist – men belonging to another class than the nobility – was now of the first importance in a campaign. It was felt, with regret, that the value of the individual, which had been the soul of the small and admirably organized bands of mercenaries, would suffer from these novel means of destruction, which did their work at a distance;

and there were *condottieri* who opposed to the utmost the introduction at least of the musket, which had been lately invented in Germany. We read that Paolo Vitelli, while recognizing and himself adopting the cannon, put out the eyes and cut off the hands of the captured *schioppettieri* of the enemy, because he held it unworthy that a gallant, and it might be noble, knight should be wounded and laid low by a common, despised foot soldier. On the whole, however, the new discoveries were accepted and turned to useful account, till the Italians became the teachers of all Europe, both in the building of fortifications and in the means of attacking them. Princes like Federigo of Urbino and Alfonso of Ferrara acquired a mastery of the subject compared to which the knowledge even of Maximilian I appears superficial. In Italy, earlier than elsewhere, there existed a comprehensive science and art of military affairs; here, for the first time, that impartial delight is taken in able generalship for its own sake which might, indeed, be expected from the frequent change of party and from the wholly unsentimental mode of action of the *condottieri*. During the Milano-Venetian war of 1451 and 1452, between Francesco Sforza and Jacopo Piccinino, the headquarters of the latter were attended by the scholar Gian Antonio Porcello dei Pandoni, commissioned by Alfonso of Naples to write a report of the campaign. It is written, not in the purest, but in a fluent Latin, a little too much in the style of the humanistic bombast of the day, is modelled on Caesar's *Commentaries*, and interspersed with speeches, prodigies and the like. Since for the past hundred years it had been seriously disputed whether Scipio Africanus or

Hannibal was the greater, Piccinino through the whole book must needs be called Scipio and Sforza Hannibal. But something positive had to be reported, too, respecting the Milanese army; the sophist presented himself to Sforza, was led along the ranks, praised highly all that he saw, and promised to hand it down to posterity. Apart from him the Italian literature of the day is rich in descriptions of wars and strategic devices, written for the use of educated men in general as well as of specialists, while the contemporary narratives of northerns, such as the *Burgundian War* by Diebold Schilling, still retain the shapelessness and matter-of-fact dryness of a mere chronicle. The greatest dilettante who has ever treated in that character of military affairs, Machiavelli, was then busy writing his *Arte della Guerra*. But the development of the individual soldier found its most complete expression in those public and solemn conflicts between one or more pairs of combatants which were practised long before the famous 'Challenge of Barletta' (1503). The victor was assured of the praises of poets and scholars, which were denied to the northern warrior. The result of these combats was no longer regarded as a divine judgement, but as a triumph of personal merit, and to the minds of the spectators seemed to be both the decision of an exciting competition and a satisfaction for the honour of the army or the nation.

It is obvious that this purely rational treatment of warlike affairs allowed, under certain circumstances, of the worst atrocities, even in the absence of a strong political hatred, as, for instance, when the plunder of a city had been promised to the troops. After the forty days devastation of Piacenza, which Sforza was compelled to permit to his soldiers (1447), the town long stood empty, and at last had to be peopled by force. Yet outrages like these were nothing compared with the misery which was afterwards brought upon Italy by foreign troops, and most of all by the Spaniards, in whom perhaps a touch of oriental blood, perhaps familiarity with the spectacles of the Inquisition, had unloosed the devilish element of human nature. After seeing them at work at Prato, Rome and elsewhere, it is not easy to take any interest of the higher sort in Ferdinand the Catholic and Charles V, who knew what these hordes were, and yet unchained them. The mass of documents which are gradually brought to light from the Cabinets of these rulers will always remain an important source of historical information; but from such men no fruitful political conception can be looked for.

The Papacy

The papacy and the dominions of the Church are creations of so peculiar a kind that we have hitherto, in determining the general characteristics of Italian states, referred to them only occasionally. The deliberate choice and adaptation of political expedients, which gives so great an interest to the other states, is what we find least of all at Rome, since here the spiritual power could constantly conceal or supply the defects of the temporal. And what fiery trials did this state undergo in the fourteenth and the beginning of the fifteenth century, when the papacy was led captive to Avignon! All, at first, was thrown into confusion; but the pope had money, troops and a great statesman and general, the Spaniard Albornoz, who again brought the ecclesiastical state into complete subjection. The danger of a final dissolution was still greater at the time of the schism, when neither the Roman nor the French pope was rich enough to reconquer the newly lost state; but this was done under Martin V, after the unity of the Church was restored, and done again under Eugenius IV, when the same danger was renewed. But the ecclesiastical state was and remained a thorough anomaly among the powers of Italy; in and near Rome itself, the papacy was defied by the great families of the Colonna, Orsini, Savelli and Anguilara; in Umbria, in the Marches and in Romagna, those civic republics had almost ceased to exist, for whose devotion the papacy had showed so little gratitude; their place had been taken by a crowd of princely dynasties, great or small, whose loyalty and obedience signified little. As self-dependent powers, standing on their own merits, they have an interest of their own; and from this point of view the most important of them have already been discussed.

Nevertheless, a few general remarks on the papacy can hardly be dispensed with. New and strange perils and trials came upon it in the course of the fifteenth century, as the political spirit of the nation began to lay hold upon it on various sides, and to draw it within the sphere of its action. The least of these dangers came from the populace or from abroad; the most serious had their ground in the characters of the popes themselves.

Let us, for this moment, leave out of consideration the countries beyond the Alps. At the time when the papacy was exposed to mortal danger in Italy, it neither received nor could receive the slightest assistance either from France, then under Louis XI, or from England, distracted by the Wars of the Roses, or from the then disorganized Spanish monarchy, or from Germany, but lately betrayed at the Council of Basel. In Italy itself there was a certain number of instructed and even uninstructed people whose national vanity was flattered by the Italian character of the papacy; the personal interests of very many depended on its having and retaining this character; and vast masses of the people still believed in the virtue of the papal blessing and consecration; among them notorious transgressors like Vitelozzo Vitelli, who still prayed to be absolved by Alexander VI, when the pope's son had him strangled. But all these grounds of sympathy put together would not have sufficed to save the papacy from its enemies, had the latter been really in earnest, and had they known how to take advantage of the envy and hatred with which the institution was regarded.

And at the very time when the prospect of help from without was so small, the most dangerous symptoms appeared within the papacy itself. Living, as it now did, and acting in the spirit of the secular Italian principalities, it was compelled to go through the same dark experiences as they; but its own exceptional nature gave a peculiar colour to the shadows.

As far as the city of Rome itself is concerned, small account was taken of its internal agitations, so many were the popes who had returned after being expelled by popular tumult, and so greatly did the presence of the Curia minister to the interests of the Roman people. But Rome not only displayed at times a specific anti-papal radicalism, but in the most serious plots which were then contrived, gave proof of the working of unseen hands from without. It was so in the case of the conspiracy of Stefano Porcari against Nicholas V (1453), the very pope who had done most for the prosperity of the city. Porcari aimed at the complete overthrow of the papal authority, and had distinguished accomplices, who, though their names are not handed down to us, are certainly to be looked for among the Italian governments of the time. Under the pontificate of the same man, Lorenzo Valla concluded his famous declamation against the gift of Constantine with the wish for the speedy secularization of the states of the Church.

The Catilinarian gang, with which Pius II had to contend (1460), avowed with equal frankness their resolution to overthrow the government of the priests, and its leader, Tiburzio, threw the blame on the soothsayers, who had fixed the accomplishment of his wishes for this very year. Several of the chief men of Rome, the Prince of Taranto and the *condottiere* Jacopo Piccinino were accomplices and supporters of Tiburzio. Indeed, when we think of the booty which was accumulated in the palaces of wealthy prelates – the conspirators had the Cardinal of Aquileia especially in view – we are surprised that, in an almost unguarded city, such attempts were not more frequent and more successful. It was not without reason that Pius II preferred to reside anywhere rather than in Rome, and even Paul II was exposed to no small anxiety through a plot formed by some discharged abbreviators, who, under the command of Platina, besieged the Vatican for twenty days. The papacy must sooner or later have fallen a victim to such enterprises, if it had not stamped out the aristocratic factions under whose protection these bands of robbers grew to a head.

This task was undertaken by the terrible Sixtus IV. He was the first pope who had Rome and the neighbourhood thoroughly under his control, especially after his successful attack on the House of Colonna, and consequently, both in his Italian policy and in the internal affairs of the Church, he could venture to act with a defiant audacity, and to set at nought the complaints and threats to summon a Council which arose from all parts of Europe. He supplied himself with the necessary funds by simony, which suddenly grew to unheard-of proportions, and which extended from the appointment of cardinals down to the granting of the smallest favours. Sixtus himself had not obtained the papal dignity without recourse to the same means.

A corruption so universal might sooner or later bring disastrous consequences on the Holy See, but they lay in the uncertain future. It was otherwise with nepotism, which threatened at one time to destroy the papacy altogether. Of all the *nipoti*, Cardinal Pietro Riario enjoyed at first the chief and almost exclusive favour of Sixtus. He soon drew upon him the eyes of all Italy, partly by the fabulous luxury of his life, partly through the reports which were current of his irreligion and his political plans. He bargained with Duke Galeazzo Maria of Milan (1473) that the latter should become King of Lombardy, and then aid him with money and troops to return to Rome and ascend the papal throne; Sixtus, it appears, would have voluntarily yielded to him. This plan, which, by making the papacy hereditary, would have ended in the secularization of the papal state, failed through the sudden death of Pietro. The second *nipote*, Girolamo Riario, remained a layman, and did not seek the pontificate. From this time the *nipoti*, by their endeavours to found principalities for themselves, became a new source of confusion to Italy. It had already happened that the popes tried to make good their feudal claims on Naples in favour of their relatives! But since the failure of Calixtus III, such a scheme was no longer practicable, and Girolamo Riario, after the attempt to conquer Florence (and who knows how many other places) had failed, was forced to content himself with founding a state within the limits of the papal dominions themselves. This was justifiable in so far as Romagna, with its princes and civic despots, threatened to shake off the papal supremacy altogether, and ran the risk of shortly falling a prey to Sforza or the Venetians, when Rome interfered to prevent it. But who, at times and in circumstances like these, could guarantee the continued obedience of *nipoti* and their descendants, now turned into sovereign rulers, to popes with whom they had no further concern? Even in his lifetime the pope was not always sure of his own son or nephew, and the temptation was strong to expel the *nipote* of a precedessor and replace him with one of his own. The reaction of the whole system on the papacy itself was of the most serious character; all means of compulsion, whether temporal or spiritual, were used without scruple for the most questionable ends, and to these all the other objects of the Apostolic See were made subordinate. And when they were attained, at whatever cost of revolutions and proscriptions, a dynasty was founded which had no stronger interest than the destruction of the papacy.

At the death of Sixtus, Girolamo was only able to maintain himself in his usurped principality of Forlì and Imola by the utmost exertions of his own, and by the aid of the House of Sforza, to which his wife belonged. In the conclave (1484) which followed the death of Sixtus – that in which Innocent VIII was elected – an incident occurred which seemed to furnish the papacy with a new external guarantee. Two cardinals, who, at the same time, were princes of ruling houses, Giovanni d'Aragona, son of King Ferrante, and Ascanio Sforza, brother of the

Moor, sold their votes with the most shameless effrontery; so that, at any rate, the ruling houses of Naples and Milan became interested, by their participation in the booty, in the continuance of the papal system. Once again, in the following conclave, when all the cardinals but five sold themselves, Ascanio received enormous sums in bribes, but without cherishing the hope that at the next election he would himself be the favoured candidate.

Lorenzo the Magnificent, for his part, was anxious that the House of Medici should not be sent away with empty hands. He married his daughter Maddalena to the son of the new pope – the first who publicly acknowledged his children – Franceschetto Cibò, and expected not only favours of all kinds for his own son, Cardinal Giovanni, afterwards Leo X, but also the rapid promotion of his son-in-law. But with respect to the latter, he demanded impossibilities. Under Innocent VIII there was no opportunity for the audacious nepotism by which states had been founded, since Franceschetto himself was a poor creature who, like his father the pope, sought power only for the lowest purpose of all – the acquisition and accumulation of money. The manner, however, in which father and son practised this occupation must have led sooner or later to a final catastrophe – the dissolution of the state. If Sixtus had filled his treasury by the sale of spiritual dignities and favours, Innocent and his son, for their part, established an office for the sale of secular favours, in which pardons for murder and manslaughter were sold for large sums of money. Out of every fine 150 ducats were paid into the papal exchequer, and what was over to Franceschetto. Rome, during the latter part of this pontificate, swarmed with licensed and unlicensed assassins; the factions, which Sixtus had begun to put down, were again as active as ever; the pope, well guarded in the Vatican, was satisfied with now and then laying a trap, in which a wealthy misdoer was occasionally caught. For Franceschetto the chief point was to know by what means, when the pope died, he could escape with well-filled coffers. He betrayed himself at last, on the occasion of a false report (1490) of his father's death; he endeavoured to carry off all the money in the papal treasury, and when this proved impossible, insisted that, at all events, the Turkish prince, Djem, should go with him, and serve as a living capital, to be advantageously disposed of, perhaps to Ferrante of Naples. It is hard to estimate the political possibilities of remote periods, but we cannot help asking ourselves the question, if Rome could have survived two or three pontificates of this kind. Even with reference to the believing countries of Europe, it was imprudent to let matters go so far that not only travellers and pilgrims, but a whole embassy of Maximilian, King of the Romans, were stripped to their shirts in the neighbourhood of Rome, and that envoys had constantly to turn back without setting foot within the city.

Such a condition of things was incompatible with the conception of power and its pleasures which inspired the gifted Alexander VI (1492–1503), and the first event that happened was the restoration, at least provisionally, of public order, and the punctual payment of every salary.

Strictly speaking, as we are now discussing phases of Italian civilization, this pontificate might be passed over, since the Borgias are no more Italian than the House of

Naples. Alexander spoke Spanish in public with Cesare; Lucrezia, at her entrance to Ferrara, where she wore a Spanish costume, was sung to by Spanish buffoons; their confidential servants consisted of Spaniards, as did also the most ill-famed company of the troops of Cesare in the war of 1500; and even his hangman, Don Micheletto, and his poisoner, Sebastian Pinzon Cremonese, seem to have been of the same nation. Among his other achievements, Cesare, in true Spanish fashion, killed, according to the rules of the craft, six wild bulls in an enclosed court. But the Roman corruption, which seemed to culminate in this family, was already far advanced when they came to the city.

What they were and what they did has been often and fully described. Their immediate purpose, which, in fact, they attained, was the complete subjugation of the pontifical state. All the petty despots, who were mostly more or less refractory vassals of the Church, were expelled or destroyed; and in Rome itself the two great factions were annihilated, the so-called Guelph Orsini as well as the so-called Ghibel-line Colonna. But the means employed were of so frightful a character that they must certainly have ended in the ruin of the papacy, had not the contemporaneous death of both father and son by poison suddenly intervened to alter the whole aspect of the situation. The moral indignation of Christendom was certainly no great source of danger to Alexander; at home he was strong enough to extort terror and obedience; foreign rulers were won over to his side, and Louis XII even aided him to the utmost of his power. The mass of the people throughout Europe had hardly a conception of what was passing in Central Italy. The only moment which was really fraught with danger – when Charles VIII was in Italy – went by with unexpected fortune, and even then it was not the papacy as such that was in peril, but Alexander, who risked being supplanted by a more respectable pope. The great, permanent and increasing danger for the papacy lay in Alexander himself, and, above all, in his son Cesare Borgia.

In the nature of the father, ambition, avarice and sensuality were combined with strong and brilliant qualities. All the pleasures of power and luxury he granted himself from the first day of his pontificate in the fullest measure. In the choice of means to this end he was wholly without scruple; it was known at once that he would more than compensate himself for the sacrifices which his election had involved, and that the simony of the seller would far exceed the simony of the buyer. It must be remembered that the vice-chancellorship and other offices which Alexander had formerly held had taught him to know better and turn to more practical account the various sources of revenue than any other member of the Curia. As early as 1494, a Carmelite, Adam of Genoa, who had preached at Rome against simony, was found murdered in his bed with twenty wounds. Hardly a single cardinal was appointed without the payment of enormous sums of money.

But when the pope in course of time fell under the influence of his son Cesare Borgia, his violent measures assumed that character of devilish wickedness which necessarily reacts upon the ends pursued. What was done in the struggle with the Roman nobles and with the tyrants of Romagna exceeded in faithlessness and barbarity even that measure to which the Aragonese rulers of Naples had already accustomed the world; and the genius for deception was also greater. The manner in which Cesare isolated his father, murdering brother, brother-in-law and other relations or courtiers, whenever their favour with the pope or their position in any other respect became inconvenient to him, is literally appalling. Alexander was forced to acquiesce in the murder of his best-loved son, the Duke of Gandia, since he himself lived in hourly dread of Cesare.

What were the final aims of the latter? Even in the last months of his tyranny, when he had murdered the *condottieri* at Sinigaglia, and was to all intents and purposes master of the ecclesiastical state (1503), those who stood near him gave the modest reply that the duke merely wished to put down the factions and the despots, and all for the good of the Church only; that for himself he desired nothing more than the lordship of the Romagna, and that he had earned the gratitude of all the following popes by riding them of the Orsini and Colonna. But no one will accept this as his ultimate design. The Pope Alexander himself, in his discussions with the Venetian ambassador, went further than this, when committing his son to the protection of Venice: 'I will see to it,' he said, 'that one day the papacy shall belong either to him or to you.' Cesare certainly added that no one could become pope without the consent of Venice, and for this end the Venetian cardinals had only to keep well together. Whether he referred to himself or not we are unable to say; at all events, the declaration of his father is sufficient to prove his designs on the pontifical throne. We further obtain from Lucrezia Borgia a certain amount of indirect evidence, in so far as certain passages in the poems of Ercole Strozza may be the echo of expressions which she as Duchess of Ferrara may easily have permitted herself to use. Here, too, Cesare's hopes of the papacy are chiefly spoken of; but now and then a supremacy over all Italy is hinted at, and finally we are given to understand that as temporal ruler Cesare's projects were of the greatest, and that for their sake he had formerly surrendered his cardinalate. In fact, there can be no doubt whatever that Cesare, whether chosen pope or not after the death of Alexander, meant to keep possession of the pontifical state at any cost, and that this, after all the enormities he had committed, he could not as pope have succeeded in doing permanently. He, if anybody, could have secularized the States of the Church, and he would have been forced to do so in order to keep them. Unless we are much deceived, this is the real reason of the secret sympathy with which Machiavelli treats the great criminal; from Cesare, or from nobody, could it be hoped that he 'would draw the steel from the wound', in other words, annihilate the papacy – the source of all foreign intervention and of all the divisions of Italy. The intriguers who thought to divine Cesare's aims, when holding out to him hopes of the kingdom of Tuscany, seem to have been dismissed with contempt.

But all logical conclusions from his premises are idle, not because of the unaccountable genius which in fact characterized him as little as it did Wallenstein, but because the means which he employed were not compatible with any large and consistent course of action. Perhaps, indeed, in the very excess of his wickedness some prospect of salvation for the papacy may have existed even without the accident which put an end to his rule.

Even if we assume that the destruction of the petty despots in the pontifical state had gained for him nothing but sympathy, even if we take as proof of his great projects the army, composed of the best soldiers and officers in Italy, with Leonardo da Vinci as chief engineer, which followed his fortunes in 1502, other facts nevertheless wear such a character of unreason that our judgement, like that of contemporary observers, is wholly at a loss to explain them. One fact of this kind is the devastation and maltreatment of the newly won state, which Cesare still intended to keep and to rule over. Another is the condition of Rome and of the Curia in the last decades of the pontificate. Whether it were that father and son had drawn up a formal list of proscribed persons, or that the murders were resolved upon one by one, in either case the Borgias were bent on the secret destruction of all who stood in their way or whose inheritance they coveted. Of this money and movable goods formed the smallest part; it was a much greater source of profit for the pope that the incomes of the clerical dignitaries in question were suspended by their death, and that he received the revenues of their offices while vacant, and the price of these offices when they were filled by the successors of the murdered men. The Venetian ambassador Paolo Capello announces in the year 1500: 'Every night four or five murdered men are discovered – bishops, prelates and others – so that all Rome is trembling for fear of being destroyed by the duke [Cesare].' He himself used to wander about Rome in the night-time with his guards, and there is every reason to believe that he did so not only because, like Tiberius, he shrank from showing his now repulsive features by daylight, but also to gratify his insane thirst for blood, perhaps even on the persons of those unknown to him.

As early as the year 1499 the despair was so great and so general that many of the papal guards were waylaid and put to death. But those whom the Borgias could not assail with open violence fell victims to their poison. For the cases in which a certain amount of discretion seemed requisite, a white powder of an agreeable taste was made use of, which did not work on the spot, but slowly and gradually, and which could be mixed without notice in any dish or goblet. Prince Djem had taken some of it in a sweet draught, before Alexander surrendered him to Charles VIII (1495), and at the end of their career father and son poisoned themselves with the same powder by accidentally tasting a sweetmeat intended for a wealthy cardinal. The official epitomizer of the history of the popes, Onofrio Panvinio, mentions three cardinals, Orsini, Ferrerio and Michiel, whom Alexander caused to be poisoned, and hints at a fourth, Giovanni Borgia, whom Cesare took into his own charge – though probably wealthy prelates seldom died in Rome at that time without giving rise to suspicions of this sort. Even tranquil scholars who had withdrawn to some provincial town were not out of reach of the merciless poison. A secret horror seemed to hang about the pope; storms and thunderbolts, crushing in walls and chambers, had in earlier times often visited and alarmed him; in the year 1500, when these phenomena were repeated, they were held to be *cosa diabolica*. The report of these events seems at last, through the well-attended jubilee of 1500, to have been carried far and wide throughout the countries of Europe, and the infamous traffic in indulgences did what else was needed to draw all eyes upon Rome. Besides the returning pilgrims, strange white-robed penitents came from Italy to the North, among them disguised fugitives from the papal state, who are not likely to have been silent. Yet none can calculate how far the scandal and indignation of Christendom might have gone before they became a source of pressing danger to Alexander. 'He would,' says Panvinio elsewhere, 'have put all the other rich cardinals and prelates out of the way, to get their property, had he not, in the midst of his great plans for his son, been struck down by death.' And what might not Cesare have achieved if, at the moment when his father died, he had not himself been laid upon a sickbed! What a conclave would that have been, in which, armed with all his weapons, he had extorted his election from a college whose numbers he had judiciously reduced by poison – and this at a time when there was no French army at hand! In pursuing such a hypothesis the imagination loses itself in an abyss.

Instead of this followed the conclave in which Pius III was elected, and, after his speedy death, that which chose Julius II – both elections the fruits of a general reaction.

Whatever may have been the private morals of Julius II, in all essential respects he was the saviour of the papacy. His familiarity with the course of events since the pontificate of his uncle Sixtus had given him a profound insight into the grounds and conditions of the papal authority.

On these he founded his own policy, and devoted to it the whole force and passion of his unshaken soul. He ascended the steps of St Peter's chair without simony and amid general applause, and with him ceased, at all events, the undisguised traffic in the highest offices of the Church. Julius had favourites, and among them were some the reverse of worthy, but a special fortune put him above the temptation to nepotism. His brother, Giovanni della Rovere, was the husband of the heiress of Urbino, sister of the last Montefeltro Guidobaldo, and from this marriage was born, in 1491, a son, Francesco Maria della Rovere, who was at the same time papal *nipote* and lawful heir to the duchy of Urbino. What Julius elsewhere acquired, either on the field of battle or by diplomatic means, he proudly bestowed on the Church, not on his family; the ecclesiastical territory, which he found in a state of dissolution, he bequeathed to his successor completely subdued, and increased by Parma and Piacenza. It was not his fault that Ferrara too was not added to the dominions of the Church. The 700,000 ducats which were stored up in the Castel Sant' Angelo were to be delivered by the governor to none but the future pope. He made himself heir of the cardinals, and, indeed, of all the clergy who died in Rome, and this by the most despotic means; but he murdered or poisoned none of them. That he should himself lead his forces to battle was for him an unavoidable necessity, and certainly did him nothing but good at a time when a man in Italy was forced to be either hammer or anvil, and when personality was a greater power than the most indisputable right. If, despite all his high-sounding 'Away with the barbarians!'

he nevertheless contributed more than any man to the firm settlement of the Spaniards in Italy, he may have thought it a matter of indifference to the papacy, or even, as things stood, a relative advantage. And to whom, sooner than to Spain, could the Church look for a sincere and lasting respect, in an age when the princes of Italy cherished none but the sacrilegious projects against her? Be this as it may, the powerful, original nature, which could swallow no anger and conceal no genuine good-will, made on the whole the impression most desirable in his situation – that of the *pontefice terribile*. He could even, with a comparatively clear conscience, venture to summon a Council to Rome, and so bid defiance to that outcry for a Council which was raised by the opposition all over Europe. A ruler of this stamp needed some great outward symbol of his conceptions; Julius found it in the reconstruction of St Peter's. The plan of it, as Bramante wished to have it, is perhaps the grandest expression of power in unity which can be imagined. In other arts besides architecture the face and the memory of the pope live on in their most ideal form, and it is not without significance that even the Latin poetry of those days gives proof of a wholly different enthusiasm for Julius than that shown for his predecessors. The entry into Bologna, at the end of the *Iter Julii Secundi*, by the Cardinal Adriano da Corneto, has a splendour of its own, and Giovan Antonio Flaminio, in one of the finest elegies, appealed to the patriot in the pope to grant his protection to Italy.

In a constitution of his Lateran Council, Julius had solemnly denounced the simony of the papal elections. After his death in 1513, the money-loving cardinals tried to evade the prohibition by proposing that the endowments and offices hitherto held by the chosen candidate should be equally divided among themselves, in which case they would have elected the best-endowed cardinal, the incompetent Raphael Riario. But a reaction, chiefly arising from the younger members of the Sacred College, who, above all things, desired a liberal pope, rendered the miserable combination futile; Giovanni Medici was elected – the famous Leo X.

We shall often meet with him in treating of the noonday of the Renaissance; here we wish only to point out that under him the papacy was again exposed to great inward and outward dangers. Among these we do not reckon the conspiracy of the Cardinals Petrucci, De Saulis, Riario and Corneto (1517), which at most could have occasioned a change of persons, and to which Leo found the true antidote in the unheard-of creation of thirty-one new cardinals, a measure which had the additional advantage of rewarding, in some cases at least, real merit.

But some of the paths which Leo allowed himself to tread during the first two years of his office were perilous to the last degree. He seriously endeavoured to secure, by negotiation, the kingdom of Naples for his brother Giuliano, and for his nephew Lorenzo a powerful North Italian state, to comprise Milan, Tuscany, Urbino and Ferrara. It is clear that the pontifical state, thus hemmed in on all sides, would have become a mere Medicean appanage, and that, in fact, there would have been no further need to secularize it.

The plan found an insuperable obstacle in the political conditions of the time. Giuliano died early. To provide for Lorenzo, Leo undertook to expel the Duke Francesco Maria della Rovere from Urbino, but reaped from the war nothing but hatred and poverty, and was forced, when in 1519 Lorenzo followed his uncle to the grave, to hand over the hard-won conquests to the Church. He did on compulsion and without credit what, if it had been done voluntarily, would have been to his lasting honour. What he attempted against Alfonso of Ferrara, and actually achieved against a few petty despots and *condottieri*, was assuredly not of a kind to raise his reputation. And this was at a time when the monarchs of the West were yearly growing more and more accustomed to political gambling on a colossal scale, of which the stakes were this or that province of Italy. Who could guarantee that, since the last decades had seen so great an increase of their power at home, their ambition would stop short of the States of the Church? Leo himself witnessed the prelude of what was fulfilled in the year 1527; a few bands of Spanish infantry appeared – of their own accord, it seems – at the end of 1520, on the borders of the pontifical territory, with a view of laying the pope under contribution, but were driven back by the papal forces. The public feeling, too, against the corruptions of the hierarchy had of late years been drawing rapidly to a head, and men with an eye for the future, like the younger Pico della Mirandola, called urgently for reform. Meantime Luther had already appeared upon the scene.

Under Adrian VI (1522–3), the few and timid improvements, carried out in the face of the great German Reformation, came too late. He could do little more than proclaim his horror of the course which things had taken hitherto, of simony, nepotism, prodigality, brigandage and profligacy. The danger from the side of the Lutherans was by no means the greatest; an acute observer from Venice, Girolamo Negro, uttered his fears that a speedy and terrible disaster would befall the city of Rome itself.

Under Clement VII the whole horizon of Rome was filled with vapours, like that leaden veil which the scirocco drew over the Campagna, and which made the last months of summer so deadly. The pope was no less detested at home than abroad. Thoughtful people were filled with anxiety, hermits appeared upon the streets and squares of Rome, foretelling the fate of Italy and of the world, and calling the pope by the name of Antichrist; the faction of the Colonna raised its head defiantly; the indomitable Cardinal Pompeo Colonna, whose mere existence was a permanent menace to the papacy, ventured to surprise the city in 1526, hoping, with the help of Charles V, to become pope then and there, as soon as Clement was killed or captured. It was no piece of good fortune for Rome that the latter was able to escape to the Castel Sant' Angelo, and the fate for which he himself was reserved may well be called worse than death.

By a series of those falsehoods, which only the powerful can venture on, but which bring ruin upon the weak, Clement brought about the advance of the Germano-Spanish army under Bourbon and Frundsberg (1527). It is certain that the Cabinet of Charles V intended to inflict on him a severe castigation, and that it could not calculate beforehand how far the zeal of its unpaid hordes would carry them. It would have been vain to attempt to enlist men in Germany without paying any bounty, if it had not been well known that Rome was the object of the expedition. It may be that the written orders to Bourbon will be found some day or other, and it is not improbable that they will prove to be worded mildly. But historical criticism will not allow itself to be led astray. The Catholic king and emperor owed it to his luck and nothing else that pope and cardinals were not murdered by his troops. Had this happened, no sophistry in the world could clear him of his share in the guilt. The massacre of countless people of less consequence, the plunder of the rest, and all the horrors of torture and traffic in human life show clearly enough what was possible in the *Sacco di Roma*.

Charles seems to have wished to bring the pope, who had fled a second time to the Castel Sant' Angelo, to Naples, after extorting from him vast sums of money, and Clement's flight to Orvieto must have happened without any connivance on the part of Spain. Whether the emperor ever thought seriously of the secularization of the States of the Church, for which everybody was quite prepared, and whether he was really dissuaded from it by the representations of Henry VIII of England, will probably never be made clear.

But if such projects really existed, they cannot have lasted long: from the devastated city arose a new spirit of reform both in Church and state. It made itself felt in a moment. Cardinal Sadoleto, one witness of many, thus writes:

> If through our suffering a satisfaction is made to the wrath and justice of God, if these fearful punishments

again open the way to better laws and morals, then is our misfortune perhaps not of the greatest ... What belongs to God He will take care of; before us lies a life of reformation, which no violence can take from us. Let us so rule our deeds and thoughts as to seek in God only the true glory of the priesthood and our own true greatness and power.

In point of fact, this critical year, 1527, so far bore fruit that the voices of serious men could again make themselves heard. Rome had suffered too much to return, even under a Paul III, to the gay corruption of Leo X.

The papacy, too, when its sufferings became so great, began to excite a sympathy half religious and half political. The kings could not tolerate that one of their number should arrogate to himself the rights of papal gaoler, and concluded (18 August 1527) the Treaty of Amiens, one of the objects of which was the deliverance of Clement. They thus, at all events, turned to their own account the unpopularity which the deeds of the imperial troops had excited. At the same time the emperor became seriously embarrassed, even in Spain, where the prelates and grandees never saw him without making the most urgent remonstrances. When a general deputation of the clergy and laity, all clothed in mourning, was projected, Charles, fearing that troubles might arise out of it, like those of the insurrection quelled a few years before, forbade the scheme. Not only did he not dare to prolong the maltreatment of the pope, but he was absolutely compelled, even apart from all considerations of foreign politics, to be reconciled with the papacy which he had so grievously wounded. For the temper of the German people, which certainly pointed to a different course, seemed to him, like German affairs generally, to afford no foundation for a policy. It is possible, too, as a Venetian maintains, that the memory of the sack of Rome lay heavy on his conscience, and tended to hasten that expiation which was sealed by the permanent subjection of the Florentines to the Medicean family of which the pope was a member. The *nipote* and new duke, Alessandro Medici, was married to the natural daughter of the emperor.

In the following years the plan of a Council enabled Charles to keep the papacy in all essential points under his control, and at one and the same time to protect and to oppress it. The greatest danger of all – secularization – the danger which came from within, from the popes themselves and their *nipoti*, was adjourned for centuries by the German Reformation. Just as this alone had made the expedition against Rome (1527) possible and successful, so did it compel the papacy to become once more the expression of a world-wide spiritual power, to raise itself from the soulless debasement in which it lay, and to place itself at the head of all the enemies of this Reformation. The institution thus developed during the latter years of Clement VII, and under Paul III, Paul IV, and their successors, in the face of the defection of half Europe, was a new, regenerated hierarchy, which avoided all the great and dangerous scandals of former times, particularly nepotism, with its attempts at territorial aggrandizement, and which, in alliance with the Catholic princes, and impelled by a new-born spiritual force, found its chief work in the recovery of what had been lost. It only existed and is only intelligible in opposition to the seceders. In this sense it can be said with perfect truth that the moral salvation of the papacy is due to its mortal enemies. And now its political position, too, though certainly under the permanent tutelage of Spain, became impregnable; almost without effort it inherited, on the extinction of its vassals, the legitimate line of Este and the house of della Rovere, the duchies of Ferrara and Urbino. But without the Reformation – if, indeed, it is possible to think it away – the whole ecclesiastical state would long ago have passed into secular hands.

Patriotism

In conclusion, let us briefly consider the effect of these political circumstances on the spirit of the nation at large.

It is evident that the general political uncertainty in Italy during the fourteenth and fifteenth centuries was of a kind to excite in the better spirits of the time a patriotic disgust and opposition. Dante and Petrarch, in their day, proclaimed loudly a common Italy, the object of the highest efforts of all her children. It may be objected that this was only the enthusiasm of a few highly instructed men, in which the mass of the people had no share; but it can hardly have been otherwise even in Germany, although in name at least that country was united, and recognized in the emperor one supreme head. The first patriotic utterances of German literature, if we except some verses of the *Minnesänger*, belong to the humanists of the time of Maximilian I and after, and read like an echo of Italian declamations. And yet, as a matter of fact, Germany had been long a nation in a truer sense than Italy ever was since the Roman days. France owes the consciousness of its national unity mainly to its conflicts with the English, and Spain has never permanently succeeded in absorbing Portugal, closely related as the two countries are. For Italy, the existence of the ecclesiastical state, and the conditions under which alone it could continue, were a permanent obstacle to national unity, an obstacle whose removal seemed hopeless. When, therefore, in the political intercourse of the fifteenth century, the common fatherland is sometimes emphatically named, it is done in most cases to annoy some other Italian state. But those deeply serious and sorrowful appeals to national sentiment were not heard again till later, when the time for unity had gone by, when the country was inundated with Frenchmen and Spaniards. The sense of local patriotism may be said in some measure to have taken the place of this feeling, though it was but a poor equivalent for it.

1. Seneca *On the Shortness of Life*
2. Marcus Aurelius *Meditations*
3. St Augustine *Confessions of a Sinner*
4. Thomas à Kempis *The Inner Life*
5. Niccolò Machiavelli *The Prince*
6. Michel de Montaigne *On Friendship*
7. Jonathan Swift *A Tale of a Tub*
8. Jean-Jacques Rousseau *The Social Contract*
9. Edward Gibbon *The Christians and the Fall of Rome*
10. Thomas Paine *Common Sense*
11. Mary Wollstonecraft *A Vindication of the Rights of Woman*
12. William Hazlitt *On the Pleasure of Hating*
13. Karl Marx & Friedrich Engels *The Communist Manifesto*
14. Arthur Schopenhauer *On the Suffering of the World*
15. John Ruskin *On Art and Life*
16. Charles Darwin *On Natural Selection*
17. Friedrich Nietzsche *Why I am So Wise*
18. Virginia Woolf *A Room of One's Own*
19. Sigmund Freud *Civilization and Its Discontents*
20. George Orwell *Why I Write*

21. Confucius *The First Ten Books*
22. Sun-tzu *The Art of War*
23. Plato *The Symposium*
24. Lucretius *Sensation and Sex*
25. Cicero *An Attack on an Enemy of Freedom*
26. *The Revelation of St John the Divine* and *The Book of Job*
27. Marco Polo *Travels in the Land of Kubilai Khan*
28. Christine de Pizan *The City of Ladies*
29. Baldesar Castiglione *How to Achieve True Greatness*
30. Francis Bacon *Of Empire*
31. Thomas Hobbes *Of Man*
32. Sir Thomas Browne *Urne-Burial*
33. Voltaire *Miracles and Idolatry*
34. David Hume *On Suicide*
35. Carl von Clausewitz *On the Nature of War*
36. Søren Kierkegaard *Fear and Trembling*
37. Henry David Thoreau *Where I Lived, and What I Lived For*
38. Thorstein Veblen *Conspicuous Consumption*
39. Albert Camus *The Myth of Sisyphus*
40. Hannah Arendt *Eichmann and the Holocaust*

41. Plutarch *In Consolation to his Wife*
42. Robert Burton *Some Anatomies of Melancholy*
43. Blaise Pascal *Human Happiness*
44. Adam Smith *The Invisible Hand*
45. Edmund Burke *The Evils of Revolution*
46. Ralph Waldo Emerson *Nature*
47. Søren Kierkegaard *The Sickness unto Death*
48. John Ruskin *The Lamp of Memory*
49. Friedrich Nietzsche *Man Alone with Himself*
50. Leo Tolstoy *A Confession*
51. William Morris *Useful Work v. Useless Toil*
52. Frederick Jackson Turner *The Significance of the Frontier in American History*
53. Marcel Proust *Days of Reading*
54. Leon Trotsky *An Appeal to the Toiling, Oppressed and Exhausted Peoples of Europe*
55. Sigmund Freud *The Future of an Illusion*
56. Walter Benjamin *The Work of Art in the Age of Mechanical Reproduction*
57. George Orwell *Books v. Cigarettes*
58. Albert Camus *The Fastidious Assassins*
59. Frantz Fanon *Concerning Violence*
60. Michel Foucault *The Spectacle of the Scaffold*

61. Lao Tzu *Tao Te Ching*
62. *Writings from the Zen Masters*
63. Thomas More *Utopia*
64. Michel de Montaigne *On Solitude*
65. William Shakespeare *On Power*
66. John Locke *Of the Abuse of Words*
67. Samuel Johnson *Consolation in the Face of Death*
68. Immanuel Kant *An Answer to the Question: 'What is Enlightenment?'*
69. Joseph de Maistre *The Executioner*
70. Thomas De Quincey *Confessions of an English Opium Eater*
71. Arthur Schopenhauer *The Horrors and Absurdities of Religion*
72. Abraham Lincoln *The Gettysburg Address*
73. Karl Marx *Revolution and War*
74. Fyodor Dostoyevsky *The Grand Inquisitor*
75. William James *On a Certain Blindness in Human Beings*
76. Robert Louis Stevenson *An Apology for Idlers*
77. W. E. B. Du Bois *Of the Dawn of Freedom*
78. Virginia Woolf *Thoughts on Peace in an Air Raid*
79. George Orwell *Decline of the English Murder*
80. John Berger *Why Look at Animals?*

81. Chuang Tzu *The Tao of Nature*
82. Epictetus *Of Human Freedom*
83. Niccolò Machiavelli *On Conspiracies*
84. René Descartes *Meditations*
85. Giacomo Leopardi *Dialogue Between Fashion and Death*
86. John Stuart Mill *On Liberty*
87. Charles Darwin *Hosts of Living Forms*
88. Charles Dickens *Night Walks*
89. Charles Mackay *Some Extraordinary Popular Delusions*
90. Jacob Burckhardt *The State as a Work of Art*
91. George Eliot *Silly Novels by Lady Novelists*
92. Charles Baudelaire *The Painter of Modern Life*
93. Sigmund Freud *The 'Wolfman'*
94. Theodor Herzl *The Jewish State*
95. Rabindranath Tagore *Nationalism*
96. Vladimir Ilyich Lenin *Imperialism*
97. Winston Churchill *We Will All Go Down Fighting to the End*
98. Jorge Luis Borges *The Perpetual Race of Achilles and the Tortoise*
99. George Orwell *Some Thoughts on the Common Toad*
100. Chinua Achebe *An Image of Africa*

THE STORY OF PENGUIN CLASSICS

Before 1946 . . . 'Classics' are mainly the domain of academics and students; readable editions for everyone else are almost unheard of. This all changes when a little-known classicist, E. V. Rieu, presents Penguin founder Allen Lane with the translation of Homer's *Odyssey* that he has been working on in his spare time.

1946 Penguin Classics debuts with *The Odyssey*, which promptly sells three million copies. Suddenly, classics are no longer for the privileged few.

1950s Rieu, now series editor, turns to professional writers for the best modern, readable translations, including Dorothy L. Sayers's *Inferno* and Robert Graves's unexpurgated *Twelve Caesars*.

1960s The Classics are given the distinctive black covers that have remained a constant throughout the life of the series. Rieu retires in 1964, hailing the Penguin Classics list as 'the greatest educative force of the twentieth century.'

1970s A new generation of translators swells the Penguin Classics ranks, introducing readers of English to classics of world literature from more than twenty languages. The list grows to encompass more history, philosophy, science, religion and politics.

1980s The Penguin American Library launches with titles such as *Uncle Tom's Cabin*, and joins forces with Penguin Classics to provide the most comprehensive library of world literature available from any paperback publisher.

1990s The launch of Penguin Audiobooks brings the classics to a listening audience for the first time, and in 1999 the worldwide launch of the Penguin Classics website extends their reach to the global online community.

The 21st Century Penguin Classics are completely redesigned for the first time in nearly twenty years. This world-famous series now consists of more than 1300 titles, making the widest range of the best books ever written available to millions – and constantly redefining what makes a 'classic'.

The Odyssey continues . . .